The Road to NYPD Retirement

(2019 Edition)

A tax and retirement planning resource for active and retired NYPD members

PETER THOMANN, EA, CFP®, CDFA®

The Road to NYPD Retirement
(2019 Edition)

Copyright © 2019 by Peter Thomann, EA, CFP®, CDFA®

All rights reserved. In accordance with the US Copyright Act of 1976, the scanning, copying, uploading, and electronic sharing of any part of this book without the permission of the author constitute unlawful piracy and the theft of the author's intellectual property.

ISBN 978-0-578-44502-1

Published by:
Thomann Tax Inc.

Introduction

The purpose of this book is to provide the retiring and retired NYPD member with a basic knowledge of tax and retirement planning in order to make well informed financial decisions. Retiring from the NYPD today is very different from 30 years ago. The modern-day NYPD retiring member is faced with many decisions that must be made and often these decisions are irrevocable. There are decisions of when to retire, election of final withdrawal, New York City Deferred Compensation Plan distributions, rollovers, pension options, tax issues, Union Annuity Plan distributions, etc. This book is not meant to provide all the answers to these difficult decisions, but hopefully will provide the reader with a solid understanding of the tax and retirement planning issues.

Abbreviations

NYCPPF	New York City Police Pension Fund	PPA	Pension Protection Act of 2006
		VSF	Variable Supplement Fund
FAS	Final Average Salary	VSF-DROP	Variable Supplement Fund-Deferred Retirement Option Plan
NYCDCP	NYC Deferred Compensation Plan		
ITHP	Increased Take Home Pay	SSB	Social Security Benefit
ITHP-NYC	Increased Take Home Pay-NYC	SSO	Social Security Offset
ADR	Accidental Disability Retirement	TCJA	Tax Cuts & Jobs Act
ODR	Ordinary Disability Retirement	QCD	Qualified Charitable Distribution
ASF	Annuity Savings Fund	RMD	Required Minimum Distribution

Disclaimer: The information and examples provided in this book are illustrative and may or may not apply to the reader's situation. The material presented should not be construed as financial and/or tax advice. Reasonable efforts have been made to ensure the accuracy of the material. Any significant corrections or revisions will be posted to www.thomanntax.com.

Contents

1. NYPD Pension Tier 2 1
2. NYPD Pension Tier 3 67
3. NYPD Pension & Divorce 99
4. NYC Deferred Compensation Plan 105
5. Union Annuity Plan 129
6. IRA & Roth IRA 133
7. Social Security 149
8. Taxes, Distribution Planning, & RMDs 159
9. Advanced Tax & Retirement Planning 177
10. Who to Turn to for Advice 195
11. Case Studies 201
    About the Author 219

CHAPTER 1
NYPD Pension Tier 2

The idea of retiring from the NYPD after 20 years of service is very appealing. Yes, there may be a few members who were disciplined savers throughout their careers that are able to ride off into the sunset and be fully retired. For the most part, NYPD members who retire after 20 years are moving on to a second career or to a less stressful job. As NYPD members get closer to their 20th anniversary they begin to analyze the advantages and disadvantages of retiring from the NYPD. For some, the decision is very simple and requires little analysis; the NYPD member retires at the 20th anniversary and never looks back. For others, the decision is not that simple due to the difficulty in obtaining a well-paying job, significant family financial obligations, divorce, debt, etc. The purpose of this chapter is to provide the pre-NYPD retiree with a better understanding of how the Tier 2 Police Pension is calculated at the 20-year retirement and beyond 20 years. When it comes to trying to decide whether to retire or not from the NYPD; knowledge is critical. Pre-retirees should learn as much as possible in order to make a more informed and educated retirement decision.

Defined Benefit

The NYPD pension is considered a defined benefit pension and is funded by both the NYPD employee and by the City Of New York. A significant advantage of the defined benefit plan for NYC Police Pension Fund (NYCPPF) members is that the investment risk is the responsibility of NYC. In other words, the NYCPPF Board have the task of investing the pension assets in order to ensure that a benefit will be available for pensioners. NYCPPF members do not have to make any investment decisions; it is all done for them.

This defined benefit will be a critical component of a retiree's overall retirement funding mechanism. Ideally, NYPD retirees will have four sources of funds for retirement available for their use: defined benefit (pension), Social Security, retirement accounts (457(b), 401(k), IRA, etc.) and personal savings. With proper planning and disciplined saving, many NYPD retirees will be able to live comfortably in their retirement years.

Required Amount

When an individual is hired by the NYPD and becomes a participating member of the NYCPPF they are assigned a specific contribution rate. The contribution rate (varies by age at appointment) is a certain percentage of pensionable earnings that are required to be contributed to the NYCPPF. These contributions are "required" for the first twenty years of service. Even though the contributions are required, members can elect to opt out of contributing and receive a reduced pension benefit. The required contributions made by the member over their 20-year career and the interest earned on the contributions determine the required amount. The required amount is different for each NYCPPF member due to different contribution rates, salary history, overtime, promotions, etc.

Table #1 displays the contribution rate based on the age of the NYCPPF member on the date of appointment.

Increased-Take-Home-Pay

The Increased-Take-Home-Pay (ITHP) provision is associated with the required amount. ITHP may also be referred to as the employer's "pick-up". Simply stated, the ITHP provision is the portion of the member's contribution rate that NYC pays or picks-up. For example, a NYCPPF Tier 2 member is hired at age 22 and is assigned a contribution rate of 7.65%. Under the current ITHP rules, NYC will contribute 5% of the 7.65%. As a result, the member's contribution rate is reduced to 2.65%, which results in an increase of take-home pay. For the member to receive an unreduced pension benefit, this member would be required to contribute 2.65% of earnings for a twenty-year period.

Table #2 displays the contribution rate based on the age of the NYCPPF member on the date of appointment reduced by the ITHP provision.

Chapter 1: NYPD Pension Tier 2

TABLE #1
NYCPPF Contribution/Assigned Rate

Appointment date age	Rate
21	7.85%
22	7.65%
23	7.50%
24	7.30%
25	7.15%
26	6.95%
27	6.80%
28	6.65%
29	6.45%
30	6.30%
31	6.15%
32	6.00%
33	5.85%
34	5.65%
35	5.50%
36	5.35%
37	5.20%
38	5.05%
39	4.90%

TABLE #2

NYCPPF Contribution/Assigned Rate less ITHP

Appointment date age	Rate	ITHP-NYC	Actual member rate
21	7.85%	5%	2.85%
22	7.65%	5%	2.65%
23	7.50%	5%	2.50%
24	7.30%	5%	2.30%
25	7.15%	5%	2.15%
26	6.95%	5%	1.95%
27	6.80%	5%	1.80%
28	6.65%	5%	1.65%
29	6.45%	5%	1.45%
30	6.30%	5%	1.30%
31	6.15%	5%	1.15%
32	6.00%	5%	1.00%
33	5.85%	5%	0.85%
34	5.65%	5%	0.65%
35	5.50%	5%	0.50%
36	5.35%	5%	0.35%
37	5.20%	5%	0.20%
38	5.05%	5%	0.05%
39	4.90%	5%	0.00%

Basic Contributions - NYCPPF Member

The basic contributions made by the pension fund member are contributed on a federal pre-tax basis but are subject to FICA (Social Security and Medicare taxes) and NYS/NYC taxes. The following is an example of a pension fund member who has a basic contribution rate of 2.15% (7.15% assigned contribution rate – 5% ITHP-NYC).

Chapter 1: NYPD Pension Tier 2

- Bi-weekly paycheck = $3,846.15
- Contribution rate = 2.15%
- $3,846.15 x .0215 = $82.69

The $82.69 is deposited into the NYCPPF member's Annuity Savings Fund (ASF) account and earns interest. The ASF is a critical aspect of a member's calculated pension and will be reviewed later.

ITHP - NYCPPF Member

The NYCPPF Tier 2 member has the option (ITHP waiver) to contribute the additional 5%. The additional 5% contributed by the member is deposited into their ASF account in the same manner as the basic pension contributions. The additional 5% contributions are made on a federal pre-tax basis but are subject to FICA taxes and NYS/NYC taxes. The following is an example of a pension fund member who has a basic contribution rate of 2.15% but has elected to contribute an additional 5%.

- Bi-weekly paycheck = $3,846.15
- Contribution rate = 2.15% + 5.00%
- $3,846.15 x .0715 = $274.99

The $274.99 is deposited into the pension fund member's ASF account and earns interest.

50% Additional Pension Contributions - NYCPPF Member

Besides the regular contributions and the ITHP contributions, a NYCPPF Tier 2 member may also elect to contribute funds known as 50% additional pension contributions. Members that elect this option contribute an additional 50% of their contribution rate. For example, a member with a contribution rate of 7.5% (23 years old at appointment) would contribute 3.75%. These 50% contributions are subject to both federal and NYS/NYC taxes. In other words, the 50% funds are contributed on an after-tax basis. These after-tax funds are deposited into the member's ASF account and earn interest.

ITHP- NYC Contribution

Many NYCPPF Tier 2 pension fund members understand the ITHP provision based on the member's contributions, but few understand how the ITHP works based on NYC's contribution of the ITHP. From March 1976 through Sept 2000, the ITHP rate was 2.5%, which means NYC was contributing 2.5% of a pension fund member's earnings into an account. This account can be referred to as the ITHP-NYC account. Every NYCPPF Tier 2 member has an ITHP-NYC account that contains these NYC contributions. From October 1st, 2000 to present, NYC added another 2.5% for a total of 5%. The 5% contributions made by NYC are not deposited into the pension fund member's ASF account, but into the member's ITHP-NYC account. In general, if a member completes exactly 20 years of service, the ITHP contributed by NYC is part of his/her Service pension. If a pension fund member completes more than 20 years of service, the ITHP-NYC account is generally factored into the Service pension as an additional benefit. If a pension fund member is granted an Accidental Disability Retirement (ADR) pension, the ITHP-NYC account is also factored into the ADR pension as an additional benefit but calculated differently from a Service pension.

Assume a NYCPPF member was hired on January 1st, 2001 at age 25 with a contribution rate of 7.15% and does not elect the ITHP waiver for the entire 20-year period. If the pension fund member completes exactly 20 years of service, the member will receive 50% of final average salary due to the 5% ITHP-NYC contribution. If the pension fund member decides to stay on the job after 20 years of service and continues to contribute 2.15%, the member will begin to accumulate an excess. The 5% ITHP-NYC contribution then becomes an added pension benefit.

Annuity Savings Fund (ASF) Account

Every NYCPPF Tier 2 member has an ASF account. The ASF account consists of the contributions made by the member via basic contributions, ITHP, 50% additional, "buy backs", etc. Funds contributed into the ASF account currently earn 8.25% interest. The balance of a member's ASF account at retirement determines if the member has a shortage or excess (also referred to as an overage). The pension a member ultimately receives is partly based on the amount in their ASF account. Simply put, the greater the ASF balance results in a larger pension to the retiree.

The following is an example of a 35-year-old NYCPPF member contributing the ITHP waiver and the 50% additional.

Chapter 1: NYPD Pension Tier 2

- Age when hired = 25
- Contribution rate = 7.15%
- Current annual earnings = $125,000

Reviewing Table #3, the member contributed $10,718.75 more than was required and reduced current taxable earnings from $125,000 to $116,062.50.

TABLE #3

Pension Contributions Summary

Item	Rate %	$ Amount Contributed	Before-tax or After-tax
Member rate	2.15%	$2,687.50	Before-tax
ITHP waiver	5.00%	$6,250.00	Before-tax
50% additional	3.575%	$4,468.75	After-tax
Total	10.725%	$13,406.25	

Deciding whether to elect the ITHP waiver and/or the 50% additional is a personal choice and often depends on what the member can afford. As previously reviewed, an excess in a member's ASF account is generally a result of the member contributing more than the required amount through the ITHP waiver and/or the 50% additional. At retirement, the excess can be withdrawn, rolled over, or left with the NYCPPF for an increased pension. Many NYCPPF members are unaware of their ASF account balances and may be doing themselves a disservice by not taking advantage of an opportunity to earn a substantial rate of return (8.25%) on their money. Members who have an excess ASF balance understand the power of compounding interest when electing the ITHP waiver and the 50% additional. Graph #1 displays the power of compounding interest along with ongoing ITHP waiver and 50% additional contributions compared with contributing only the required (basic) amount.

- Contribution rate = 7.15%
- ITHP waiver = Yes
- 50% additional = Yes
- Annual salary from years 15 through 19 = $110,000
- ASF balance at end of 14 years of service = $90,000

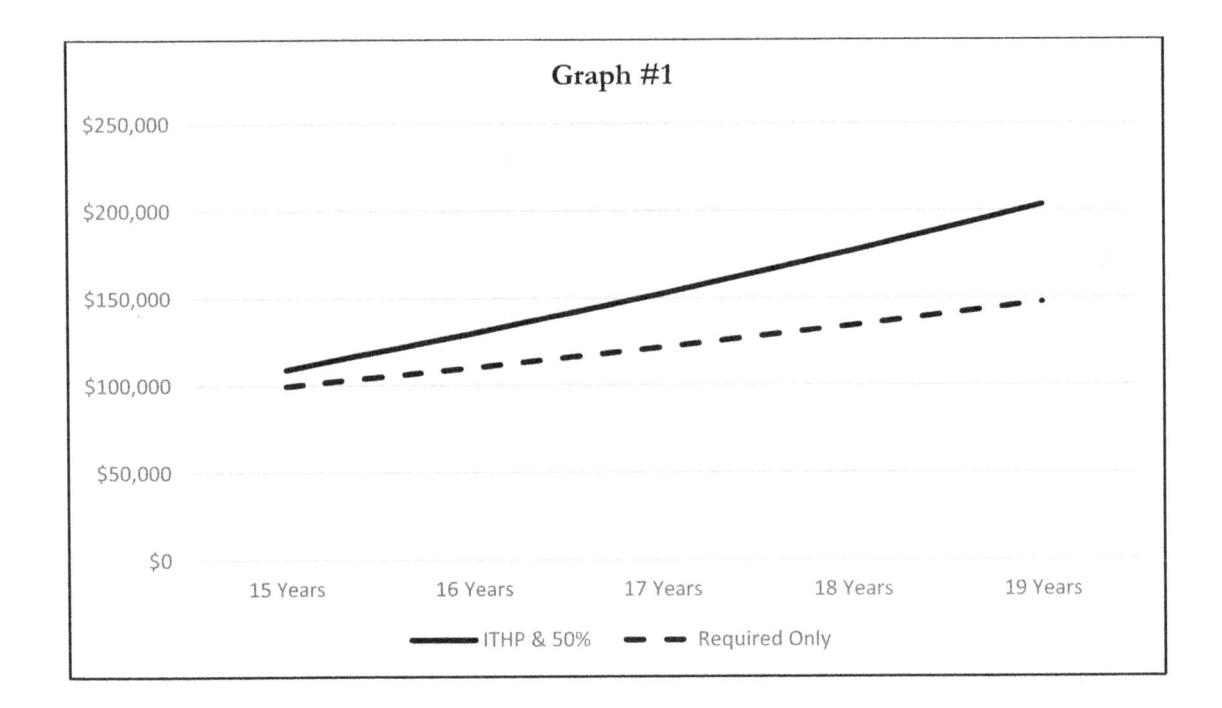

Graph #1

(Line graph showing ASF balance growth from 15 to 19 years of service. Solid line "ITHP & 50%" rises from ~$110,000 to ~$203,000. Dashed line "Required Only" rises from ~$100,000 to ~$147,000.)

A review of Graph #1 indicates that the member who contributed both the ITHP waiver and the 50% additional had an ending balance of $203,302. The member who contributed only the required amount had an ending balance of $147,721. Let's see what happens if we continue the same process for another 5 years.

Chapter 1: NYPD Pension Tier 2

- Contribution rate = 7.15%
- ITHP waiver = Yes
- 50% additional = Yes
- Annual salary from years 20 through 24 = $120,000
- ASF balance for member contributing ITHP waiver and 50% additional at end of 19 years of service = $203.302
- ASF balance for member electing to contribute the basic amount only at end of 19 years of service = $147,721

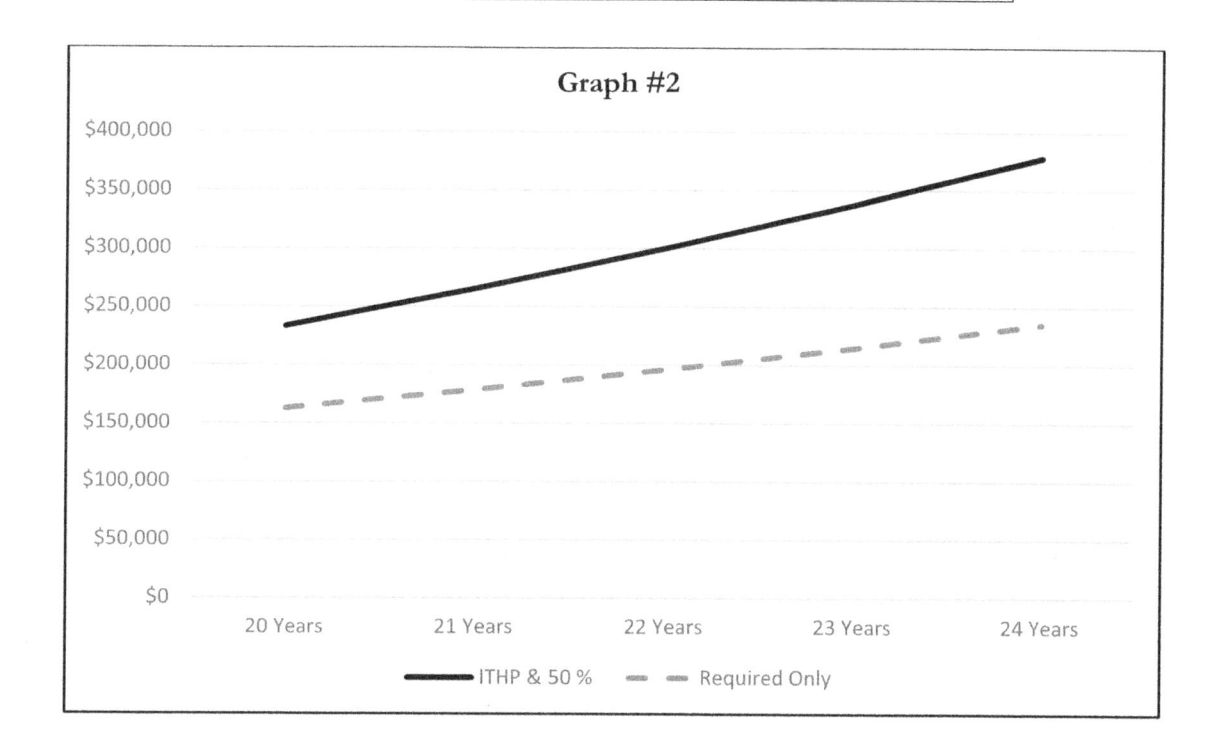

Graph #2

A review of Graph #2 indicates that the member who contributed both the ITHP waiver and the 50% additional had an ending balance of $378,036. The member who contributed only the required amount had an ending balance of $234,786.

Shortage and Excess

A shortage occurs when a member's ASF balance is less than their required amount. An excess occurs when a member's ASF balance is more than their required amount. The following are causes of a shortage.

- Pension loan(s)
- Service transfers and buybacks
- Stopping pension contributions
- Contract settlement (back pay)

Is it possible to make up a shortage? Yes, there are methods available that increase a member's ASF account and therefore reduce or eliminate the shortage. Generally, the methods are lump-sum contributions, ITHP waiver, and 50% additional contributions.

Author's Tip

In the author's opinion, contributing as much money as possible to the ASF provides the retiring member with greater flexibility when making retirement decisions. NYCPPF Tier 2 members often ask in what order, based on affordability, should contributions be made to either the NYCPPF or the NYC Deferred Compensation Plan? Tier 2 members should consider contributing the basic contributions, ITHP, and 50% additional to the NYCPPF before the NYC Deferred Compensation Plan.

Final Average Salary

The final average salary (FAS) is the starting point in determining the pension of a retiring NYCPPF member. The FAS consists of pensionable earnings: salary, night shift differential, holiday pay, overtime, longevity, etc. It should be noted that the longevity at 20 years of service is pensionable at the completion of 25 years of service. Members retiring at 20 years of service and less than 25 years of service calculate pensionable longevity at the 10-year level.

There are different definitions of FAS depending on date of appointment. For members who have an appointment date prior to July 1st, 2000 there are three different methods available to calculate FAS.

- Final 12 months
- Final 36 months
- Three consecutive calendar years

Members appointed after July 1st, 2000 through June 30th, 2009 are only permitted to use the final 12 months as FAS.

The FAS may be limited if pensionable earnings exceed the prior year or years by 20%. Table #4 is an example of the final 12 months FAS accounting for the "20% rule." The final 12 months immediately precedes the retirement date and does not have to be a calendar year.

TABLE #4			
FAS- Final 12 months 20% Rule			
12 Month Period	Pensionable Earnings	Earnings Limit	Pensionable Earnings for FAS
Period 1	$135,000	$144,000	$135,000
Period 2	$120,000	N/A	N/A

Table #5 is an example of the three consecutive calendar years calculation for FAS without the pensionable earnings being limited. Table #6 is an example of the pensionable earnings being limited. In order to correctly calculate the three consecutive calendar years, the member needs to account for the two previous calendar years.

TABLE #5			
FAS- Three Consecutive Years 20% Rule			
Year	Pensionable Earnings	Earnings Limit	Pensionable Earnings for FAS
1	$155,000	$165,000	$155,000
2	$145,000	$148,800	$145,000
3	$130,000	$139,800	$130,000
4	$118,000	N/A	N/A
5	$115,000	N/A	N/A
Three Year Average = $143,333			

TABLE #6

FAS- Three Consecutive Years 20% Rule

Year	Pensionable Earnings	Earnings Limit	Pensionable Earnings for FAS
1	$155,000	$160,200	$155,000
2	$142,000	$140,400	$140,400
3	$125,000	$134,400	$125,000
4	$109,000	N/A	N/A
5	$115,000	N/A	N/A
Three Year Average = $140,133				

The Importance of "Retirement Age"

Before performing any pension calculation/estimate, the NYCPPF member should understand "retirement age". To perform the most accurate pension estimate, the retirement age of the pre-retiree determines which annuity factor to use. The NYCPPF defines retirement age as the closest birthday to the pre-retiree's retirement date. For example, if a pre-retiree's birthday is on 6/30/65 and his retirement date is 11/30/19, the age used for pension calculations is 54 years old. Another example, if the pre-retiree's birthday is on 6/30/65 and his retirement date is 12/31/19, the age for pension calculations is 55 years old. What difference does it make whether the pre-retiree is 54 or 55 years old? A 54-year-old has a Service annuity factor of 10.858 while the 55-year-old has a Service annuity factor of 10.666. The annuity factor is used to determine the value of an excess or shortage and the ITHP-NYC, if applicable.

For example, assume a pre-retiree NYCPPF member has an excess of $300,000 in their ASF account. For the 54-year-old, the Service annuity value of the excess is equal to $27,629 while the Service annuity value of the excess is equal to $28,126 for the 55-year-old.

Author's Tip

For help with FAS average calculations use the Tax & RP App iPhone app. The app has four averaging calculators: 12 months 20% limit, 3-year average 10% limit, 3-year average 20% limit, and 5-year average 10% limit.

Basic 20 Year NYPD Pension Calculation

Calculating a 20-year Service retirement NYPD pension benefit is simple and much of the calculation is based on the member's ASF balance as compared to the member's required amount. The ASF consists of a member's contributions and the interest earned on the contributions. For a member to receive exactly 50% of FAS, their ASF must equal their required amount.

> **Assumptions**
> - Years of Service = 20
> - FAS = $100,000
> - Member's required amount = $95,000
> - Member's ASF balance = $95,000
> - Annual pension benefit = $50,000
>   (2.5% x FAS x years of service)

Basic 20 Year NYPD Pension Calculation - Shortage

If a NYCPPF member has less than the required amount in their ASF account, a shortage exists, and the pension will be less than 50% of the FAS.

> **Assumptions**
> - 20-year service retirement
> - Retirement age = 45
> - Required amount = $90,000
> - Member's ASF balance = $60,000
> - Shortage = $30,000
> - Member's FAS = $100,000
>
> **Calculations**
> - 50% of FAS = $50,000
> - Annuity value of shortage = $2,453
> - Annual pension benefit = $47,547

The pension formula for the above example is: 2.5% x FAS x years of service – annuity value of shortage.

Basic 20 Year NYPD Pension Calculation - Excess

If a NYCPPF member has more than the required amount in their ASF account, an excess exists, and the pension will be more than 50% of the FAS.

> **Assumptions**
> - 20-year service retirement
> - Retirement age = 45
> - Required amount = $90,000
> - Member's ASF balance = $130,000
> - Excess = $40,000
> - Member's FAS = $100,000
>
> **Calculations**
> - 50% of FAS = $50,000
> - Annuity value of excess = $3,271
> - Annual pension benefit = $53,271

The pension formula for the above example is: 2.5% x FAS x years of service + annuity value of excess.

Beyond 20 Years NYPD Pension Calculations

There are significant monetary benefits for an NYPD member to remain on the job after 20 years of service. The basic pension formula for a member with more than 20 years of service is as follows.

- 50% of FAS
- Plus, 1/60th of earnings after 20th anniversary
- Plus, annuity value of ITHP-NYC contributions after 20th anniversary
- Plus, annuity value of the excess over the required amount <u>or</u> less the annuity value of a shortage

The following is an example of a NYCPPF member who retired after 22 years of service and had an excess in their ASF account.

Chapter 1: NYPD Pension Tier 2

Assumptions
- 22-year service retirement
- Retirement age = 47
- Required amount = $90,000
- Member's ASF balance = $160,000
- Excess = $70,000
- Member's FAS = $110,000
- Earnings from 20 to 22 years = $220,000

Calculations
- 50% of FAS = $55,000
- Value of 1/60ths = $3,667
- Estimated annuity value of ITHP-NYC benefit = $1,002
- Value of excess = $5,844
- Annual pension benefit = $65,513

The following is an example of a NYCPPF member who retired after 30 years of service and had an excess in their ASF account.

Assumptions
- 30-year service retirement
- Retirement age = 55
- Required amount = $90,000
- Member's ASF balance = $190,000
- Excess = $100,000
- Member's FAS = $120,000
- Earnings from 20 to 30 years = $1,100,000

Calculations
- 50% of FAS = $60,000
- Value of 1/60ths = $18,333
- Estimated annuity value of ITHP-NYC benefit = $8,247
- Value of excess = $9,376
- Annual pension = $95,956

Value of 1/60ths Calculation

Calculating the value of the 1/60ths benefit requires the average salary over 20 years. The average salary is divided by 60 and then multiplied by the number of years beyond 20 years of service. For example, a NYCPPF member completed 23.431 years of service and had an average salary of $147,209.19 after 20 years. The $147,209.19 is divided by 60 and then multiplied by 3.431. The result is a $1/60^{th}$ annual benefit of $8,417.91. An alternative method to estimate the value of the $1/60^{th}$ benefit is to determine the total amount of earnings from after the 20th anniversary until retirement. After the total earnings are determined, divide by 60. Technically, if an individual were to retire after 20 years and one day, the amount of money earned for that one day beyond 20 years would receive a $1/60^{th}$ benefit. In other words, a NYCPPF member does not need to complete a full year to earn the $1/60^{th}$ benefit.

Note: the $1/60^{th}$ benefit continues until retirement, the 30-year cap was removed by legislation in February 2002.

Value of Excess Pension Benefit Calculation

Calculating the value of an excess is easy to determine. The pre-retiree NYCPPF member only needs to know the excess value and an annuity factor based on retirement age and type of retirement. The required amount and the excess can be obtained from a member's NYCPPF Annual Pension Statement. The excess is calculated by subtracting the required amount from the member's ASF balance. The annuity factor can be obtained from table #7.

The following is an example of the pension value of an excess calculation.

- Excess amount = $75,000
- Age at retirement = 50
- Excess divided by annuity factor = pension value

Calculation
- $75,000/11.551
- Excess pension value = $6,493

TABLE #7

1985 Basis Annuity Factor
(Service Retirement Appointment Date After 8-19-1985)

Retirement Age	Annuity Factor
40	12.748
41	12.654
42	12.556
43	12.452
44	12.343
45	12.228
46	12.107
47	11.979
48	11.844
49	11.701
50	11.551
51	11.391
52	11.222
53	11.043
54	10.858
55	10.666
56	10.469
57	10.266
58	10.056
59	9.839
60	9.612
61	9.376
62	9.131
63	8.876

Value of ITHP-NYC Pension Benefit Calculation

NYCPPF members who retire with more than 20 years of service receive this added pension benefit. This calculation is more involved, and it may be easier for a pre-retiree to estimate this benefit when planning for retirement. The pre-retiree NYCPPF member would need to know the following information in order to estimate the ITHP-NYC pension benefit: earnings from the 20th anniversary till retirement (for a Service retirement), ITHP-NYC contribution rate, interest rate factor, and annuity factor. Currently, the ITHP-NYC contribution rate is 5%, interest rate earned is 8.25%, and the same annuity factors in table #7 are used. The following is an example of an <u>estimated</u> ITHP-NYC pension benefit calculation.

- 22-year service retirement
- Retirement age = 45
- Earnings 21st year = $110,000
- Earnings 22nd year = $115,000

Calculations
- $110,000 x .05 = $5,500
- $5,500 x 1.0825 + $5,750 = $11,704
- $11,704/1000 x 81.78 = $957
- Value of <u>estimated</u> NYC ITHP pension benefit = $957

20 vs. 25 vs. 30 Year Service Retirement

As NYCPPF members get close to 20 years of service, they often ask about the benefit of staying to 25 years of service. In most cases, there is a significant monetary difference between a 20-year pension and a 25-year pension. In order to complete an analysis of 20 vs. 25 vs. 30, the pre-retiree would need to make some assumptions about their projected earnings and pension contributions. The following lengthy example will attempt to show the difference between a 20-year pension, a 25-year pension, and a 30-year pension.

20 Year Service Retirement Pension

Assumptions

- 20 years of service
- Retirement age = 45
- FAS = $110,000
- Required amount = $90,000
- Member's ASF balance = $125,000
- Excess = $35,000

Calculations

- 50% of FAS = $55,000
- Value of excess = $2,862
- Total annual pension benefit after 20 years = $57,862

25 Year Service Retirement Pension

Assumptions

- 1% FAS increase per year ($111,100, $112,211, $113,333, $114,466, & $115,611)
- An additional $2,000 to FAS based on longevity
- Member elected the ITHP waiver for the entire five-year period
- 25 years of service
- Retirement age = 50
- FAS = $117,611
- Required amount = $90,000
- Member's ASF balance = $233,505
- Excess = $143,505

Calculations

- 50% of FAS = $58,806
- Value of 1/60ths = $9,445 ($566,721/60)
- <u>Estimated</u> annuity value of ITHP-NYC benefit = $2,888
- Value of excess = $12,423
- Total annual pension benefit after 25 years = $83,562

30 Year Service Retirement Pension

Assumptions
- 1% FAS increase per year ($118,787, $119,975, $121,175, $122,386, & $123,610)
- Member elected the ITHP waiver for the entire five-year period
- 30 years of service
- Retirement age = 55
- FAS = $123,610
- Required amount = $90,000
- Member's ASF balance = $398,092
- Excess = $308,092

Calculations
- 50% of FAS = $61,805
- Value of 1/60ths = $19,544 ($1,172,654/60)
- <u>Estimated</u> annuity value of ITHP-NYC benefit = $6,232
- Value of excess = $28,885
- Total annual pension benefit after 30 years = $116,466

Next, the pre-retiree may want to analyze the length of time it would take to make up not receiving the pension benefit at 20 years - also known as a breakeven point. The breakeven means the point at which you would have received the same total amount of money from the NYCPPF no matter when you retired. Many retirees do a similar calculation when deciding on whether to take a Social Security Retirement benefit at 62 years old or delaying to a later age. Using the figures from the example; table #8 displays the result.

Chapter 1: NYPD Pension Tier 2

TABLE #8

Breakeven Analysis 20 vs. 25 vs. 30

Age	20 Year Retirement	25 Year Retirement	30 Year Retirement
46	$57,862	$0	$0
47	$57,862	$0	$0
48	$57,862	$0	$0
49	$57,862	$0	$0
50	$57,862	$0	$0
51	$57,862	$83,562	$0
52	$57,862	$83,562	$0
53	$57,862	$83,562	$0
54	$57,862	$83,562	$0
55	$57,862	$83,562	$0
56	$57,862	$83,562	$116,466
57	$57,862	$83,562	$116,466
58	$57,862	$83,562	$116,466
59	$57,862	$83,562	$116,466
60	$57,862	$83,562	$116,466
61	$57,862	$83,562	$116,466
Total received	$925,792	$919,182	$698,796
62	$57,862	$83,562	$116,466
63	$57,862	$83,562	$116,466
64	$57,862	$83,562	$116,466
65	$57,862	$83,562	$116,466
Total received	$1,157,240	$1,253,430	$1,164,660
66	$57,862	$83,562	$116,466
67	$57,862	$83,562	$116,466
68	$57,862	$83,562	$116,466
Total received	$1,330,826	$1,504,116	$1,514,058

TABLE #9
Summary of 20 vs. 25 vs. 30 Example

Item	20 yr.	25 yr.	30 yr.
Annual pension benefit	$57,862	$83,562	$116,466
Percentage increase	N/A	44%	39%
Retirement age	45	50	55
Breakeven point (age) vs. 20 yr. retirement	N/A	61	65
Breakeven point (age) vs. 25 yr. retirement	N/A	N/A	68

The example determines that remaining on the job until 25 years of service resulted in an approximately 44% larger annual pension benefit than the 20-year retirement. The length of time to make up the difference of staying until 25 years of service was a little over 11 years. In other words, the 25-year pension begins to surpass the 20-year pension around the 11th or 12th year of retirement. The 30-year retirement resulted in an approximately 39% larger annual pension benefit than the 25-year retirement and an approximately 101% larger annual pension benefit than the 20-year retirement. The length of time to make up the difference of staying until 30 years of service was about 13 years when compared to the 25-year retirement and about 10 years when compared to the 20-year retirement. Determining the breakeven point should not be the only criteria when an individual is trying to decide whether to retire after 20 years of service. Other factors to consider may include: job satisfaction, life expectancy, overall health, interest earned on ASF account, desire for a second career, ability to contribute to the NYC Deferred Compensation Plan, etc.

Author's Tip

For help with a breakeven analysis use the Tax & RP App iPhone app. The app has a basic breakeven calculator that is easy to use.

Pension Calculations-Appointment Date Prior to August 19th, 1985

Many pre-1985 NYCPPF members assume that their pensions are calculated using more favorable factors than post-1985 members. Technically, pensions for pre-1985 members are calculated using two different methods and the member receives the higher benefit of the two. Table #10 compares the two methods when calculating a service retirement.

Chapter 1: NYPD Pension Tier 2

Assumptions
- Appointment date 7/1/1985
- Retirement age = 60
- FAS = $150,000
- ASF balance = $300,000
- Required amount = $120,000
- Excess amount = $180,000
- Final withdrawal amount = $288,000

TABLE #10

Pension Calculation Pre-1985 Appointment Date

Item	Pre- 8/19/85 Method	Post 8/19/85 Method
50% of FAS	$75,000	$75,000
60ths	$32,000	$32,000
ITHP-NYC	$13,669	$16,646
Value of excess	$15,378	$18,727
Total pension	$136,047	$142,373
"Cost" of withdrawal	($24,605)	($29,963)
Adjusted pension	$111,442	$112,410

As indicated in table #10, the pre-1985 member would receive the pension as calculated using the post 1985 method since it is the higher of the two calculations.

Pension Loan

NYCPPF members with more than three years of service are permitted to borrow money from their pension account (ASF). Prior to electing to take a pension loan, the member should carefully review the various rules in order to prevent taxability. This is one area where a member can easily make a mistake and very often the mistake is irrevocable or difficult to fix. Ideally, it is best for a member not to take a pension loan during their career in order to receive the highest pension benefit possible at retirement. Of course, the ideal is not the reality for most members and a pension loan becomes a necessity at some point due to unexpected expenses, family financial obligations, etc. Prior to requesting a pension loan, the member may want to review any other available methods to receive the needed funds. For example, it may make better sense for a member to finance the purchase of a new car using a car dealer's low financing rates rather than taking a pension loan. A significant disadvantage of taking a pension loan is that the monies removed no longer receive the 8.25% rate of return for funds in a member's ASF account. As many members are aware, taking a pension loan(s) results in a shortage and if not corrected via the ITHP waiver and/or 50% additional results in a reduced pension at retirement. A few guidelines regarding pension loans.

- Are other loan sources available? Home equity, family, NYC Deferred Compensation Plan, Finest Federal Credit Union, etc.
- If a member borrows taxable contributions and the repayment schedule is greater than five years, the loan becomes taxable and may be subject to a 10% penalty. The 10% penalty is accessed for a member who is less than 59 ½ years old.
- Carefully complete the NYCPPF Loan Application form. If you are not sure about what to enter on the form, ask someone at the NYCPPF who is familiar with pension loans.

There is an Internal Revenue Code exception (§72(p)(2)(B)(ii)) available to the five-year repayment schedule for taxable pension loans. This exception may allow a participant to extend the five-year repayment schedule to 15 years in order to purchase a primary residence. For members considering this exception it is strongly recommended that you consult a qualified and knowledgeable tax professional. Incorrectly using this exception may result in IRS scrutiny (audit).

Outstanding Pension Loan at Retirement

In general, retiring with an outstanding pension loan that consists of taxable funds often results in unfavorable tax consequences. The taxable portion of the loan will be considered a taxable distribution subject to taxes and generally a 10% penalty. Depending on the amount of the outstanding loan, the taxes owed can become very significant. When a loan is outstanding at retirement, the "age 50" exception does not apply, and the taxable portion of the loan is subject to the 10% early distribution penalty if less than 59 ½ years old. To determine if the outstanding loan can be rolled over, the retiree should review the 1099-R that was issued and consult with a knowledgeable tax preparer.

Final Withdrawal (Final loan)

At retirement, pension fund members will have to decide whether to elect to take a final withdrawal (often referred to as the final loan) from their ASF account. This is one decision that many members have great difficulty in determining what is best for their situation. There is no perfect answer when trying to decide and the decision should be based on personal circumstances.

Very simply, electing to receive the final withdrawal results in a lower pension benefit while not electing results in a higher pension benefit. How much a member's pension decreases, or increases is based on various factors, such as: appointment date, age at retirement, and type of retirement. Currently, the NYCPPF permits retiring members the option to receive a full final withdrawal or a partial final withdrawal. A full final withdrawal would consist of 90% of the required amount and any excess funds available (including non-taxable). A partial final withdrawal would consist of a portion of the required amount, a portion of the excess, excess only, etc.

Final Withdrawal Calculation Examples

Example #1 is a basic calculation of a retiring member who has elected to take the full final withdrawal.

Assumptions
- 20-year service retirement
- Retirement age = 45
- FAS = $110,000
- Required amount = $90,000
- Member's ASF account = $125,000
- Member's excess amount = $35,000
- Full final withdrawal available = $116,000

Calculations
- 50% of FAS = $55,000
- Value of excess = $2,862 ($35,000/12.228)
- Annual pension before full final withdrawal = $57,862 ($55,000 + 2,862)
- Annual pension reduced by full final withdrawal = $9,486 ($116,000/12.228)
- Annual pension after full final withdrawal = $48,376 ($57,862 − 9,486)
- Annual pension received is 44% of FAS

Note: if the member in the above example decided to elect a partial final withdrawal of only the excess funds; the annual pension benefit would be equal to 50% of the FAS.

Example #2 is a retiring member who has a significant excess and has elected to take the full final withdrawal.

Assumptions
- 30-year service retirement
- Retirement age = 55
- FAS = $150,000
- Required amount = $120,000
- Earnings from 20-30 years = $1,100,000
- Member's ASF account = $325,000
- Member's excess amount = $205,000
- Full final withdrawal available = $313,000

Calculations
- 50% of FAS = $75,000
- Value of 1/60ths = $18,333 ($1,100,000/60)
- <u>Estimated</u> annuity value of ITHP-NYC benefit = $9,000
- Value of excess = $19,220 ($205,000/10.666)
- Total annual pension before full final withdrawal = $121,553 ($75,000 + 18,333 + 9,000 + 19,220)
- Annual pension reduced by full final withdrawal =
  1. 90% of required amount/10.666 = $10,126
  2. Excess amount/10.666 = $19,220
      $29,346 ($10,126 + 19,220)
- Annual pension after full final withdrawal = $92,207 ($121,553 − 29,346)
- Annual pension received is 61% of FAS

Example #3 is a retiring member (using the same dollar figures as example 2) who has a significant excess and has elected to take a partial final withdrawal of the excess funds only.

Assumptions
- 30-year service retirement
- Retirement age = 55
- FAS = $150,000
- Required amount = $120,000
- Earnings from 20-30 years = $1,100,000
- Member's ASF account = $325,000
- Member's excess amount = $205,000
- Full final withdrawal available = $313,000

Calculations
- 50% of FAS = $75,000
- Value of 1/60ths = $18,333 ($1,100,000/60)
- <u>Estimated</u> annuity value of ITHP-NYC benefit = $9,000
- Value of excess = $19,220 ($205,000/10.666)
- Total annual pension before full final withdrawal = $121,553 ($75,000 + 18,333 + 9,000 + 19,220)
- Annual pension reduced by partial final withdrawal = $19,220 ($205,000/10.666)
- Annual pension after partial final withdrawal = $102,313 ($121,553 − 19,220)
- Annual pension benefit received is 68% of FAS

Final Withdrawal Advantages and Disadvantages

When a retiring member elects to take a final withdrawal, the funds withdrawn become their own asset. Since the retiring member now owns the funds, he or she can spend it and/or invest it as they wish (there are various income rules tax rules regarding the final withdrawal which will be reviewed later). As previously reviewed, electing the final withdrawal results in a lower annual pension benefit. This lower annual pension benefit continues throughout the life of the retiree and beneficiary, if applicable.

For a member who does not elect a final withdrawal, the NYCPPF keeps the money, interest is no longer credited to the member, and the member no longer has access or ownership of the money. Not electing the final withdrawal results in a larger annual pension benefit for the life of the retiree and beneficiary, if applicable.

Electing a final withdrawal affords the retiree the <u>opportunity</u> to earn interest/appreciation on the withdrawn funds. The appreciation of the withdrawn funds is critical because the true purchasing power of the annual pension benefit received will become significantly reduced as the retiree ages. Currently, NYCPPF Tier 2 retirees receive a small cost-of-living-adjustment (COLA) after certain conditions are met. The COLA, 50% of CPI, is only based on the first $18,000 of pension benefit and has a minimum of 1% and a maximum of 3%. Therefore, the minimum COLA adjustment is $180 per year to a maximum of $540 per year. Due to the limited COLA, the annual pension benefit will not keep pace with inflation over a retiree's lifetime. For example, a retiree who receives an annual pension benefit of $50,000 may begin to realize the significant effects of inflation erosion 5-10 years after retirement. Five years after retirement, the $50,000 annual pension benefit will be worth $44,193 based on an inflation factor of 2.5%. Ten years after retirement, the $50,000 annual pension benefit will be worth $39,060 based on an inflation factor of 2.5%. Obviously, if a retiree lives through a period of high inflation, the true purchasing power of the annual pension benefit will become even more reduced.

> **Author's Tip**
>
> For help with the final withdrawal analysis use the Tax & RP App iPhone app. The app has a Pension Analyzer calculator that may help members with the decision of whether to take the final withdrawal.

Rolling Over the Final Withdrawal

This is another topic that some pre-retirees have difficulty in understanding and properly executing. Ideally, a member that elects the final withdrawal will rollover the taxable portion of the final withdrawal (in order to prevent immediate taxation) into a new retirement plan. The general rule regarding distributions from the new retirement plan is that distributions are taxable and subject to a 10% penalty if received prior to 59 ½ years old (there are exceptions to the 10% penalty). If a member decides to not rollover the taxable portion of the final withdrawal it will be considered a taxable distribution and will be subject to tax and a 10% penalty if less than 50 years old at retirement. Table #11 summarizes.

TABLE #11			
Final Withdrawal Taxable & 10% Penalty			
	IRS Age	*Taxable*	*10% Penalty*
Not rolling over taxable final withdrawal	Less than 50	Yes	Yes
Not rolling over taxable final withdrawal	50 and over	Yes	No
Rolling over taxable final withdrawal	Any age	No	No
Distributions from new retirement plan	N/A	Yes	Yes, if less than 59 ½ years old (exceptions)

Pension Protection Act of 2006

Prior to the Pension Protection Act of 2006 (PPA), if a retiring individual less than 55 years old were to take a distribution from a defined benefit plan, they would be subject to the 10% early distribution penalty. In general, the PPA changed the age from 55 to age 50 for retiring NYPD members. Technically, the retiring NYPD member does not have to be 50 but will be 50 in the calendar year of the distribution. For example, assume a retiring NYPD member is 49 years old at a retirement date of March 31, but his birthday is December 1. The retiring member would qualify for the age 50 exception since he will attain age 50 during the calendar year of the distribution. There may be an instance when the 10% early distribution penalty will still apply to retiring members at age 50 to 59 ½ years old. For example, if a 52-year-old individual retired with an outstanding loan from the NYCPPF, the 10% early distribution penalty would apply. To clarify this rule further, assume that a 50-year-old pension fund member received a pension loan of $50,000 at age 48. At age 50, the outstanding loan balance is $32,000. If the NYPD member decided to retire at age 50, the $32,000 outstanding loan balance would be subject to the 10% early distribution penalty.

As per the PPA, the exception does not apply if the member rolls over distributions from the NYCPPF into an IRA or defined contribution plan. However, the Defending Public Safety Employees Retirement Act changed this provision of the PPA.

The Defending Public Safety Employees Retirement Act

Before reviewing the type of retirement plans available for the taxable final withdrawal, pre-retirees should be very familiar with this exception. The Defending Public Safety Employees Retirement Act (referred to as the "age 50 rule"), was signed by President Obama on June 29, 2015, and creates some interesting tax planning strategies for the retired NYPD member. In general, this act was created for the benefit of federal employees (federal police, customs, border protection, air traffic controllers, etc.), but due to its wording, a benefit was created for certain public safety officers (NYPD retirees).

As previously reviewed, the PPA allowed the 50-year-old or older NYPD pre-retiree a "one-shot" deal at retirement to cash out NYCPPF distributions and not be subject to the 10% early distribution penalty. If the NYCPPF pre-retiree did not cash out the distribution, but instead rolled the funds into an IRA or retirement plan, then the general rule of 59½ years old would apply in order to receive distributions without penalty (unless an exception applies).

With the enactment of the Defending Public Safety Employees Retirement Act, the retiring NYPD member can roll over a distribution (final withdrawal) from the NYCPPF into a governmental defined contribution plan and still maintain the age 50 rule as per IRC § 72(t)(10).

> **Author's Tip**
>
> Who is a qualified public safety officer for the purpose of qualifying for the IRC § 72(t)(10) exception? A qualified public safety employee is an employee of a state or of a political subdivision of a state (such as The City of New York) whose principal duties include services requiring specialized training in police protection, firefighting services, or emergency medical services for any area within the jurisdiction of the state or the political subdivision of the state.

Rolling Over to a New Retirement Plan

Deciding on what retirement plan to rollover the final withdrawal into is another area of difficulty for pre-retirees. This may be a difficult decision for many pre-retirees due to the process of rolling over the money and the number of choices. There are two methods available when rolling over the final withdrawal. The first method is a direct rollover from the NYCPPF to a new retirement plan. The direct rollover is accomplished at retirement by correctly completing the paperwork provided by the NYCPPF. The direct rollover results in the funds being transferred electronically from the NYCPPF to the member's retirement plan. The second method is a direct payment to the retiring member. For a member who elects the direct payment method, 20% tax withholding is withheld from the check(s). In order to prevent taxation, the total amount of the taxable final withdrawal money should be rolled into the new retirement plan within 60 days of the date(s) of the check(s) received from the NYCPPF. It is recommended that prior to rolling over the money; the retiree should make copies of the checks before they are deposited. The copies of the checks should be retained in a folder that the retiree maintains for important tax/financial documents. In most cases, the direct rollover is the preferred method for members who choose to elect the final withdrawal.

The retiring member will need to decide what type of retirement plan to rollover the taxable final withdrawal. Selecting which retirement plan is based on various factors: personal preferences, investing knowledge, investment choices, etc. Currently, the following retirement plans are available for the rollover of the taxable final withdrawal.

- Individual Retirement Account (IRA)
- Roth Individual Retirement Account (Roth IRA)
- NYC Deferred Compensation Plan Pension Rollover Account (also referred to as a "Special" 401(k))
- Union Annuity Plan (in some cases)
- New employer retirement plan

Individual Retirement Account

The Individual Retirement Account (IRA) may be an option for the retiree who desires many investment choices and types and/or for the retiree seeking the safety of Certificates of Deposit (CDs). An IRA can be established at a bank, a discount brokerage firm (Charles Schwab, E*TRADE, Vanguard, etc.), or through a financial advisor. Many are not aware that IRAs can be invested in many different types of securities or financial products. An IRA may be invested in mutual funds, individual equities (stocks), CDs, bonds, etc. Depending on where the IRA is established, the retiree may have the ability to choose among thousands of investments.

Roth Individual Retirement Account

The Roth Individual Retirement Account (Roth IRA) has the same type of investing flexibility and custodian choices of the IRA. The difference between an IRA and a Roth IRA is the tax implications of rolling over the money. Correctly rolling over the taxable final withdrawal money into an IRA will result in not owing any taxes; the retiree is simply deferring the taxes. Alternatively, there is a current taxable event if the retiree rolls over the taxable final withdrawal into a Roth IRA. How much taxes would be owed depends on numerous factors: value of taxable final withdrawal, retiree's tax bracket, type of retirement (Service or ADR), etc. Table #12 compares rolling over the taxable final withdrawal into an IRA vs. a Roth IRA.

TABLE #12
Final Withdrawal IRA vs. Roth IRA

	IRA	Roth IRA
Tax filing status	Single	Single
Taxable final withdrawal	$100,000	$100,000
W2 earnings prior to retirement	$75,000	$75,000
Pension benefit from retirement to year end	$30,000	$30,000
Gross income	$105,000	$205,000
Standard deduction	$12,000	$12,000
Taxable income	$93,000	$193,000
Federal tax (2018)	$16,610	$43,450
Tax bracket (2018)	24%	32%

As table #12 indicates, the result of the retiree rolling over the taxable final withdrawal into a Roth IRA was an increased tax bracket to 32%. For a retiree considering the Roth IRA it may be worthwhile to meet with a qualified tax/financial advisor in order to fully understand the tax implications for their situation. The advantages of a Roth IRA will be reviewed in a later chapter.

NYC Deferred Compensation Plan Pension Rollover Account

The NYC Deferred Compensation Plan (NYCDCP) offers an account, often referred to as a "Special" 401(k), that permits NYCPPF members to rollover their taxable final withdrawal at retirement. The money rolled over is not comingled with any other NYCDCP retirement plans the member may have. The purpose of not comingling the retirement plans is to keep track of the original NYS tax basis when the funds were rolled over. This may be a suitable option for the retiree who likes familiarity. Many NYCPPF members have participated in the NYCDCP for years and are very familiar with the different investment choices offered.

Union Annuity Plan

In some cases, the retiring member may be able to rollover their taxable final withdrawal into their Union Annuity Plan. Many members pay little attention to their Union Annuity Plan while working, but this may be an option available at retirement. The retiring member should check with their own union in order to determine if this option is available.

New Employer Retirement Plan

For the retiree moving on to a new employer, the taxable final withdrawal may be rolled over into the new employer's retirement plan. The new employer's retirement plan would have to permit incoming rollovers and the type of the new employer's plan would also have to be reviewed. Additionally, the retiree would also have to review the investment choices offered in the new employer plan and determine if they are suitable for their overall financial situation.

Analyzing the Final Withdrawal - Annuitize

When analyzing the final withdrawal decision, many pre-retirees calculate how long they will have to live after NYPD retirement to make up the "cost" of the final withdrawal. The calculation they perform is simply the total final withdrawal divided by the cost of the final withdrawal. For example, if a retiree elects a $150,000 final withdrawal and the cost is equal to $12,267, it would take the retiree a little over 12 years to "be ahead of the game." Although this is an easy calculation to perform and understand it is generally not accurate because the retiree is not accounting for income taxes. Prior to deciding whether the pre-retiree should elect the final withdrawal, a more detailed analysis should be performed. This analysis is member specific and different factors should be considered; type of retirement, age, and tax rate of retiree. For pre-retirees who decide to not take the final withdrawal they have elected to annuitize their pension contributions over their life expectancy. The following is an example of a pre-retiree who has elected to <u>not</u> take the final withdrawal.

- Retirement age of 46
- Service retirement
- $200,000 available as a final withdrawal (before-tax)
- 20% federal tax rate

In analyzing the decision, the pre-retiree considered the $200,000 as an investment and calculated the internal rate of return (used to evaluate the attractiveness of an investment). Based on the pre-retiree's age and Service retirement, the NYCPPF will provide $16,519 per year ($1,376.61 per month) if the $200,000 is not withdrawn. Accounting for federal tax (20% flat rate), the pre-retiree will receive $13,215 per year after-tax. Using the after-tax amount ($13,215), the internal rate of return can be calculated. Table #13 displays the internal rate of return from age 47 to age 85.

TABLE #13
Internal Rate of Return (IRR)

Retirement Age	IRR
47	-93.44%
48	-70.8%
49	-51.6%
50	-37.9%
51	-28.3%
52	-21.4%
53	-16.2%
54	-12.3%
55	-9.3%
56	-6.9%
57	-5.0%
58	-3.4%
59	-2.1%
60	-1.0%
61	-0.1%

Chapter 1: NYPD Pension Tier 2

Retirement Age	IRR
62	0.7%
63	1.3%
64	1.9%
65	2.4%
66	2.8%
67	3.2%
68	3.5%
69	3.8%
70	4.1%
71	4.3%
72	4.5%
73	4.7%
74	4.9%
75	5.0%
76	5.1%
77	5.3%
78	5.4%
79	5.5%
80	5.6%
81	5.6%
82	5.7%
83	5.8%
84	5.8%
85	5.9%

Reviewing table #13 indicates that the investment (annuitizing the $200,000) is not a favorable investment during the retiree's early retirement years. In fact, in this example it takes the retiree until age 62 to "breakeven". From age 62 to age 85, the investment is positive and ultimately would provide a 5.9% return if the retiree were to live to age 85.

Analyzing the Final Withdrawal - Appreciation of Rollover Account

As reviewed earlier, the main purpose of electing the final withdrawal is to invest the money in order to attempt to keep up or surpass the cost of inflation. This is a task that some retirees have difficulty in achieving. The selection of an appropriate investment(s) should be based on a retiree's overall risk tolerance, time horizon, purpose of money, etc. There is a tremendous amount of information (too much) available to assist the retiree in selecting an appropriate investment for their situation. What type of investment(s) to select is beyond the scope of this book. Electing the final withdrawal and investing it prudently is not a get rich scheme and requires discipline and investing prowess. Quite simply, the retiree has two choices: do it on their own or hire an investment professional. For the retiree who wants to proceed on their own it may be worthwhile to read a basic investing book or take an adult education course on the principles of investing money. The hiring of an investment professional will be reviewed in a later chapter.

Table #14 displays the results of a rollover account appreciating using different rate of return assumptions.

Analyzing the Final Withdrawal - Cost vs. Appreciation

Some pre-retirees calculate how many years it will take to make more in appreciation than what the final withdrawal cost (reduction in pension). To keep this calculation basic, it is suggested that taxes are ignored. Table #15 displays, based on a 45-year-old Service retiree, how long it takes to earn more in appreciation than the annual cost ($16,356) of the final withdrawal.

Reviewing table #15 indicates that a retiree investing their rollover account and assuming a 6% appreciation rate, the result is that it would take approximately 7 years after retirement to earn more money than the cost of the final withdrawal.

This analysis can be taken a step further if a retiree compares electing the final withdrawal vs. not electing the final withdrawal and accounting for income taxes. For the retiree who does not elect the final withdrawal, their gross income increases due to the higher annual pension benefit. This higher gross income normally results in more current taxes being paid. For the retiree who elects the final withdrawal, the funds are rolled into a retirement plan and the appreciation of the account is tax deferred. Table #16 displays, based on a 45-year-old Service retiree, the results.

TABLE #14

$200,000 Taxable Final Withdrawal Rolled Over Appreciation

Years Retired	Value at 2% Appreciation	Value at 4% Appreciation	Value at 6% Appreciation	Value at 8% Appreciation
1	$204,000	$208,000	$212,000	$216,000
2	$208,080	$216,320	$224,720	$233,280
3	$212,242	$224,973	$238,203	$251,942
4	$216,486	$233,972	$252,495	$272,098
5	$220,816	$243,331	$267,645	$293,866
6	$225,232	$253,064	$283,704	$317,375
7	$229,737	$263,186	$300,726	$342,765
8	$234,332	$273,714	$318,770	$370,186
9	$239,019	$284,662	$337,896	$399,801
10	$243,799	$296,049	$358,170	$431,785
11	$248,675	$307,891	$379,660	$466,328
12	$253,648	$320,206	$402,439	$503,634
13	$258,721	$333,015	$426,586	$543,925
14	$263,896	$346,335	$452,181	$587,439
15	$269,174	$360,189	$479,312	$634,434
16	$274,557	$374,596	$508,070	$685,189
17	$280,048	$389,580	$538,555	$740,004
18	$285,649	$405,163	$570,868	$799,204
19	$291,362	$421,370	$605,120	$863,140
20	$297,189	$438,225	$641,427	$932,191

TABLE #15

$200,0000 Taxable Final Withdrawal Rollover Appreciation vs. Cost

Years Retired	2% Appreciation	4% Appreciation	6% Appreciation	8 % Appreciation
1	$4,000	$8,000	$12,000	$16,000
2	$4,080	$8,320	$12,720	**$17,280**
3	$4,162	$8,653	$13,483	$18,662
4	$4,245	$8,999	$14,292	$20,155
5	$4,330	$9,359	$15,150	$21,768
6	$4,416	$9,733	$16,059	$23,509
7	$4,505	$10,123	**$17,022**	$25,390
8	$4,595	$10,527	$18,044	$27,421
9	$4,687	$10,949	$19,126	$29,615
10	$4,780	$11,386	$20,274	$31,984
11	$4,876	$11,842	$21,490	$34,543
12	$4,973	$12,316	$22,780	$37,306
13	$5,073	$12,808	$24,146	$40,291
14	$5,174	$13,321	$25,595	$43,514
15	$5,278	$13,853	$27,131	$46,995
16	$5,383	$14,408	$28,759	$50,755
17	$5,491	$14,984	$30,484	$54,815
18	$5,601	$15,583	$32,313	$59,200
19	$5,713	$16,207	$34,252	$63,936
20	$5,827	**$16,855**	$36,307	$69,051

TABLE #16

$200,000 Taxable Final Withdrawal Rolled Over
$16,356 Cost, 5% Appreciation, & 20% flat tax rate

Years Retired	5% Appreciation	After-tax cost of final withdrawal	Gain or loss	Cumulative
1	$10,000	$13,085	-$3,085	-$3,085
2	$10,500	$13,085	-$2,585	-$5,670
3	$11,025	$13,085	-$2,060	-$7,730
4	$11,576	$13,085	-$1,509	-$9,239
5	$12,155	$13,085	-$930	-$10,168
6	$12,763	$13,085	-$322	-$10,491
7	$13,401	$13,085	**$316**	-$10,175
8	$14,071	$13,085	$986	-$9,189
9	$14,775	$13,085	$1,690	-$7,499
10	$15,513	$13,085	$2,428	-$5,071
11	$16,289	$13,085	$3,204	-$1,867
12	$17,103	$13,085	$4,018	**$2,151**
13	$17,959	$13,085	$4,874	$7,025
14	$18,856	$13,085	$5,771	$12,797
15	$19,799	$13,085	$6,714	$19,511
16	$20,789	$13,085	$7,704	$27,215
17	$21,829	$13,085	$8,744	$35,959
18	$22,920	$13,085	$9,835	$45,794
19	$24,066	$13,085	$10,981	$56,775
20	$25,270	$13,085	$12,185	$68,960

As Table #16 indicates, starting at the end of the first year retired, the retiree who selected the final withdrawal would be at a $3,085 loss based on the assumptions. At the end of retirement year seven, the retiree begins to see a gain on the final withdrawal rollover account vs. the after-tax cost of the final withdrawal. Then, at the end of retirement year 12 the cumulative column turns positive.

Summary: No Final Withdrawal vs. Final Withdrawal

TABLE #17

No Final Withdrawal vs. Final Withdrawal		
	No Final Withdrawal	*Final Withdrawal*
Annual pension	Increased	Reduced
Current income tax	Increased	Reduced
Ownership of funds	NYCPPF	Retiree
Accessibility of funds	No	Yes
Opportunity for appreciation	No	Yes
Select a beneficiary	No	Yes

After-tax Funds Distributed from the NYCPPF

Currently, the NYCPPF permits members to take a distribution of only after-tax funds at retirement. At some point, the NYCPPF will more than likely have to comply with the IRS pro-rata rule. The pro-rata rule was created by the Tax Reform Act of 1986 and is a difficult rule for many people to understand. This lack of understanding leads many people to incorrectly assume that they are being "double taxed" on their money. Basically, the pro-rata rule limits an individual's ability to withdraw after-tax (sometimes referred to as "tax-free" or "non-taxable") contributions by themselves. Many tax and financial professionals often refer to the pro-rata rule as the "cream in the coffee" rule. In other words, once cream (after-tax contributions) is poured into coffee (before-tax contributions), it is impossible to separate the cream from the coffee.

The following flowchart is provided to help pre-retirees understand how the pro-rata works. Four amounts are needed to correctly calculate the taxable and non-taxable amounts: total account balance, after-tax contributions, before-tax balance, and amount distributed.

Chapter 1: NYPD Pension Tier 2

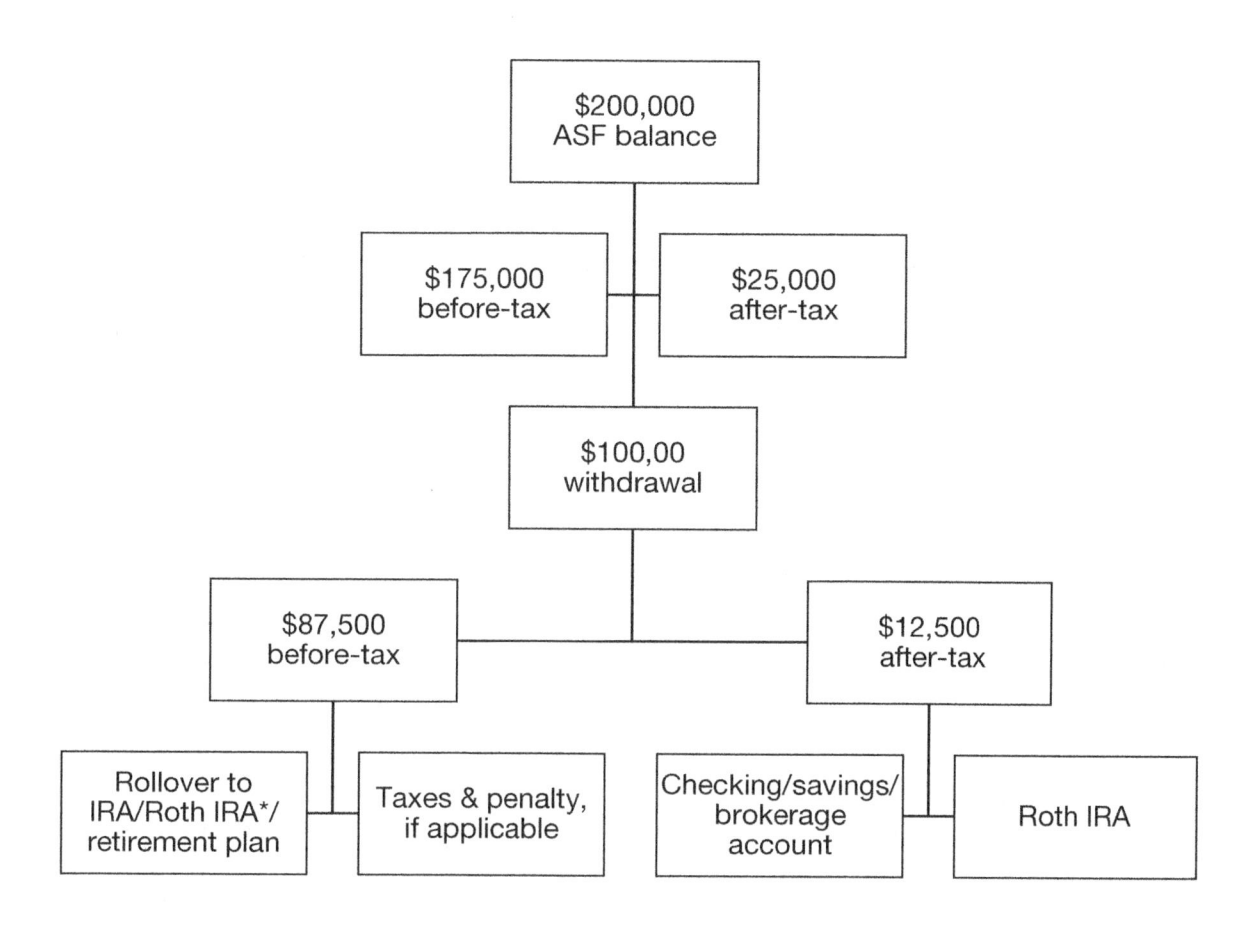

```
                    ┌─────────────────┐
                    │    $200,000     │
                    │   ASF balance   │
                    └─────────────────┘
                            │
              ┌─────────────┴─────────────┐
    ┌─────────────────┐           ┌─────────────────┐
    │    $175,000     │           │     $25,000     │
    │   before-tax    │           │    after-tax    │
    └─────────────────┘           └─────────────────┘
                            │
                    ┌─────────────────┐
                    │    $100,00      │
                    │   withdrawal    │
                    └─────────────────┘
                            │
              ┌─────────────┴─────────────┐
    ┌─────────────────┐           ┌─────────────────┐
    │     $87,500     │           │     $12,500     │
    │   before-tax    │           │    after-tax    │
    └─────────────────┘           └─────────────────┘
         │                                 │
    ┌────┴────┐                       ┌────┴────┐
┌──────────┐ ┌──────────┐        ┌──────────────┐ ┌──────────┐
│Rollover  │ │          │        │Checking/     │ │          │
│to IRA/   │ │Taxes &   │        │savings/      │ │ Roth IRA │
│Roth IRA*/│ │penalty,  │        │brokerage     │ │          │
│retirement│ │if        │        │account       │ │          │
│plan      │ │applicable│        │              │ │          │
└──────────┘ └──────────┘        └──────────────┘ └──────────┘
```

Reviewing the flowchart, a NYCPPF pre-retiree has an ASF balance of $200,000. The $200,000 balance consists of $175,000 before-tax (pre-retiree contributions and interest earned) and $25,000 of after-tax (pre-retiree contributions of after-tax funds). The pre-retiree elects a $100,000 final withdrawal at retirement. To determine the before-tax portion and the after-tax portion, a calculation is required.

- Before-tax balance divided by ASF balance $175,000/$200,000 = .875
- After-tax balance divided by ASF balance $25,000/$200,000 = .125
- Final withdrawal requested = $100,000
- $100,000 x .875 = $87,500 before-tax portion
- $100,000 x .125 = $12,500 after-tax portion

Due to the IRS's pro-rata rule, the pre-retiree will receive a portion of the before-tax funds ($87,500) and a portion of the after-tax funds ($12,500). The $87,500 (before-tax portion) can be rolled over to an IRA, Roth IRA (*subject to taxation), retirement plan, or "cashed out" subject to taxation and possibly a 10% early distribution penalty. The $12,500 (after-tax portion) can go to a checking/savings/taxable brokerage account or to a Roth IRA. After the distribution of the $100,000 to the pre-retiree, the ASF balance would be $100,000, consisting of $87,500 (before-tax) and $12,500 (after-tax). A later section reviews how the after-tax funds are recovered to avoid double taxation. It should be noted, there is an additional option available for the $100,000 distribution that is not displayed in the flowchart. The pre-retiree could roll over the entire $100,000 to an IRA, and then the IRA would have a non-taxable basis of $12,500.

The following is a more detailed example and is the **author's interpretation** of how the pro-rata rule may be implemented for a retiring NYCPPF member. Assume a 50-year-old member is retiring with the following.

- Maximum annual service pension = $120,000
- Required amount = $135,000
- ASF balance = $350,000
- Before-tax portion = $285,000
- After-tax portion = $65,000
- Excess = $215,000
- Full final withdrawal available = $336,500

The retiring member may have three choices at retirement as displayed in Table #18.

Chapter 1: NYPD Pension Tier 2

TABLE #18
Pro-rata Rule Detailed Example

Item	No Withdrawal	Excess Only	Full Withdrawal
Annual pension	$120,000	$101,387	$90,868
Monthly pension	$10,000	$8,449	$7,572
Total withdrawal amount	N/A	$215,000	$336,500
Eligible rollover amount	N/A	$175,071	$274,007
After-tax amount distributed	N/A	$39,929	$62,493
After-tax recovery amount	$65,000	$25,071	$2,507
Recovery years	30	30	30
After-tax recovered per year	$2,166.67	$835.70	$83.57

Reviewing table #18 indicates that if the retiring member elected not to withdraw any money, the pro-rata rule is not necessary, but the retired member should recover $65,000 of after-tax money over a 30-year period. If the pre-retiree were to choose excess only; $175,071 would be available for rollover (before-tax portion), $39,929 would be distributed to the retiree after-tax, and $25,071 would remain with the pension fund to be recovered over a 30-year period. Finally, if the pre-retiree were to choose full final withdrawal; $274,007 would be available for rollover (before-tax portion), $62,493 would be distributed to the retiree after-tax, and $2,507 would remain with the pension fund to be recovered over a 30-year period.

Author's Tip

For help with the IRS Pro-rata rule use the Tax & RP App iPhone app. The app has a pro-rata calculator that may help members with determining the after-tax amount distributed.

After-tax Funds not Removed from the NYCPPF

During the retirement process, some NYCPPF members decide to not take a withdrawal of their after-tax contributions. The after-tax contributions remain with the NYCPPF and the members receive a higher pension benefit. Unfortunately, for these retirees many of them may be taxed again on these after-tax contributions. Currently, the NYCPPF does not report the recovery of these after-tax contributions on the IRS 1099-R form.

The best way to explain the recovery of the non-taxable portion of the pension is by example. The following example is how the after-tax amounts should be reported on the IRS 1099-R form. Assume a 50-year-old was retired on January 1, 2019. Over the retiree's career, he contributed $50,000 of after-tax funds into his NYCPPF ASF and elected not to remove any of his contributions at retirement. Also, assume the retiree elected single-life annuity for the pension (no beneficiary and pension payments end upon the retiree's death). In this example, the recovery of the after-tax funds will be based on the simplified method and 360 monthly pension payments. The IRS 1099-R form entry for box #1 is $75,000 as a gross distribution ($6,250 per month), box #2a is a taxable amount of $73,333.33, and box #5 indicates employee contributions of $1,666.66. Even though the retiree received $75,000, he was only taxed on $73,333.33 and recovered $1,666.66 of his after-tax money for year 2019.

Since the NYCPPF does not currently account for the non-taxable portion on the IRS 1099-R form, the retiree is responsible to recover the non-taxable portion of the pension on his or her annual tax return. Based on the author's experience, very few retirees are performing the necessary calculations and are ultimately paying more income tax than required. If the retiree wants to avoid double taxation of the after-tax funds not removed at retirement, he or she will need to recover them every year a tax return is prepared until the funds are fully recovered. To recover the non-taxable portion, the retiree will need to know the amount of the after-tax funds remaining with the NYCPPF and the number of payments. Using $50,000 as an example of after-tax funds not removed at retirement, the 50-year-old retiree will then perform the following calculation.

- $50,000 / 360 = $138.88
- $138.88 x 12 payments for the year = $1,666.66

The $1,666.66 is then "deducted" on the retiree's tax return. How the $1,666,66 is deducted is not reviewed here due to the different types of tax software available. Different factors are used for the retiree who elects a multiple-lives annuity (pension payments are made to a beneficiary upon the retiree's death). For example, we'll use the same assumptions from the previous example, except the retiree has elected for his 50-year-old spouse to receive his pension upon his death. The retiree will then perform the following calculation.

Chapter 1: NYPD Pension Tier 2

- Retiree age (50) + Spouse's age (50) = 100
- $50,000 / 410 = $121.95
- $121.95 x 12 payments for the year = $1,463.41
- $1463.41 is then "deducted" on the retiree's tax return.

Table #19 displays the factors used for the recovery of after-tax funds with a pension starting date of after 1997.

TABLE #19
After-tax Recovery

Age at Pension Start Date	Single Life Pension	Combined Ages at Pension Start Date	Multiple Lives Pension
55 or under	360	110 or under	410
56-60	310	111-120	360
61-65	260	121-130	310

Terminal Leave, Yes or No?

Leading up to retirement, NYCPPF members will have to decide whether to remain on payroll while on terminal leave or receive it as a lump sum and retire earlier. For members entitled to cash overtime and are using their final 12 months for FAS, the decision to receive the terminal leave as a lump sum may be more favorable than remaining on payroll. The lump sum terminal leave payment is not a retirement plan that can be entirely rolled over but is considered wages (paycheck). The lump sum payment is subject to taxes, but since it is a paycheck the retiring member can elect to defer up to 75% into the NYCDCP 457(b) or 401(k).

Terminal Leave Lump Sum & Taxes

The terminal leave lump sum payment is subject to federal income tax, FICA (Social Security & Medicare taxes), and NYS/NYC income taxes. The federal tax withheld is a flat 22%; the IRS considers the payment a supplemental wage check. Whether a retiree is subject to Social

Security tax withholding will depend if the retiree already paid the maximum withholding to Social Security for the year of payment.

Table #20 displays the tax withholding results of an example terminal leave payout of $20,000 with no deferral to the NYCDCP, retiree has not reached the Social Security wage limit, and is a NYC resident.

TABLE #20	
Terminal Leave & Taxes	
Item	Tax
Federal tax	$4,400
Social Security tax	$1,240
Medicare tax	$290
NYS/NYC taxes	$2,200
Total taxes (based on tax year 2018)	$8,130
Net to retiree	$11,870

Terminal Leave & Remain on Payroll

For some pre-retirees it may be worthwhile to perform a breakeven analysis before making the decision to remain on payroll during terminal leave vs. terminal leave as a lump sum to retire earlier. The breakeven analysis would simply compare the two scenarios to determine how many years taking the terminal leave would be more favorable than terminal leave as a lump sum. The following is an example of remaining on payroll for terminal leave with a breakeven analysis.

Assumptions
- Retirement age = 52
- $80,000 annual pension/$72,000 pre-finalized
- $6,667 monthly/$6,000 pre-finalized
- 3 months of terminal leave money
- Annual pension increase of $1,834 due to remaining on payroll
- Maximum pension (no option) at finalization
- Finalization occurs in the 4th year

Table #21 displays the result of the breakeven analysis.

Chapter 1: NYPD Pension Tier 2

TABLE #21
Terminal Leave Breakeven Analysis

Retirement months/years	TL Lump Sum	TL Stay on Payroll	Result
Monthly pension	$6,000	$0	-$6,000
Monthly pension	$6,000	$0	-$12,000
Monthly pension	$6,000	$0	-$18,000
1	$72,000	$73,651	-$16,349
2	$72,000	$73,651	-$14,878
3	$72,000	$73,651	-$13,227
4	$106,000	$106,385	-$12,662
5	$80,000	$81,834	-$10,828
6	$80,000	$81,834	-$8,994
7	$80,000	$81,834	-$7,160
8	$80,000	$81,834	-$5,326
9	$80,000	$81,834	-$3,492
10	$80,000	$81,834	-$1,658
11	$80,000	$81,834	+$176
Total	$900,000	$900,176	
12	$80,000	$81,834	+$2,010
13	$80,000	$81,834	+$3,844
14	$80,000	$81,834	+5,678
15	$80,000	$81,834	+$7,512
Total	$1,220,000	$1,227,512	
16	$80,000	$81,834	+$9,346
17	$80,000	$81,834	+$11,180
18	$80,000	$81,834	+$13,014
19	$80,000	$81,834	+$14,848
20	$80,000	$81,834	+$16,682
Total	$1,620,000	$1,636,682	
21	$80,000	$81,834	+$18,516
22	$80,000	$81,834	+$20,350
23	$80,000	$81,834	+$22,184
24	$80,000	$81,834	+$24,018
25	$80,000	$81,834	+$25,852
Total	$2,020,000	$2,045,852	

As indicated in table #21, if the example retiree were to stay on payroll during terminal leave it would take approximately 11 years before it becomes favorable. If the example retiree were to live until 77 years old, he or she would have received $25,852 of additional pension money.

Variable Supplement Fund

Very simply, if a NYCPPF member retires (Service retirement) with 20 years of service or more they will receive the annual Variable Supplement Fund (VSF) payment. Currently, the annual VSF payment is $12,000 and is distributed to Service retirees only; Ordinary and Accidental retirees do not receive the annual VSF benefit. The annual VSF payment is taxed by the federal government, but not taxed by NYS/NYC.

VSF Deferred Retirement Option Plan

The Variable Supplement Fund Deferred Retirement Option Plan (VSF DROP) became effective on January 1st, 2002. The VSF DROP, also referred to as banked VSF, is beneficial to the NYCPPF member who decides to stay on the job past 20 years of service. Prior to 2002, the member who decided to remain on the job after 20 years of service forfeited the annual VSF payment. Now, once 20 years of service is reached and the member does not retire, the VSF begins to get "banked." Upon retirement, the NYCPPF member will need to decide what to do with the VSF DROP money. Basically, there are two choices; roll it over or distribute it. For most, the best choice would be to rollover the funds in order to avoid immediate taxation and a penalty, if applicable. The VSF DROP money has the same tax consequences as the final withdrawal as shown in table #22.

TABLE #22			
VSF DROP Taxable & 10% Penalty			
	IRS Age	Taxable	10% Penalty
Not rolling over VSF DROP	Less than 50	Yes	Yes
Not rolling over VSF DROP	50 and over	Yes	No
Rolling over VSF DROP	Any age	No	No
Distributions from new retirement plan	N/A	Yes	Yes, if less than 59 ½ years old (exceptions)

The VSF DROP money also has the same rollover options as the final withdrawal. VSF DROP money can be rolled over to the following.

- Individual Retirement Account (IRA)
- Roth Individual Retirement Account (Roth IRA)
- NYC Deferred Compensation Plan Pension Rollover Account
- Union Annuity Plan (in some cases)
- New employer retirement plan

Once the VSF DROP money is rolled over to the new retirement plan it will be subject to the distribution rules of the new retirement plan. For example, assume a 51-year-old NYCPPF member retires and rolls over the VSF DROP to an IRA and the following year takes a distribution from the IRA. In this case, the member would be subject to the 10% early distribution penalty unless an exception applies. Prior to rolling over the VSF DROP funds, the pre-retiree should be familiar with the "age 50 rule" exception, which was previously reviewed.

Accidental Disability Retirement Pension

An Accidental Disability Retirement (ADR) pension is granted to a member that is determined to be physically or mentally unable to perform as a NYC Police Officer. The disability is a result of an accidental injury in the line of duty. A NYCPPF member who retires with an ADR does not receive the annual VSF payment and generally does not receive any VSF DROP payment, if applicable. The tax implications of an ADR changed on January 1st, 2009 and have caused some confusion among retiring ADR members.

Accidental Disability Retirement Pension Tax Issues

Prior to January 1st, 2009, a NYCPPF member who received an ADR pension had an entire benefit that was federally non-taxable. After January 1st, 2009 members retiring with an ADR pension will have some of their benefit taxed by the federal government and possibly by a state government. How much will be taxed depends on total years of service, type of ADR, final or no final withdrawal, resident state, etc. The following items are currently subject to federal taxes and possibly state taxes in reference to an ADR pension.

- Value of 1/60ths benefit
- Annuitized value of member pension contributions and interest
- ITHP-NYC benefit after 20 years of service

Accidental Disability Retirement Pension Calculations

Example #1 is a basic calculation of a retiring ADR member who has elected not to take a final withdrawal.

Assumptions
- 10-year ADR
- Retirement age = 41
- Required amount = $15,000
- ASF balance = $50,000
- Final withdrawal = No
- FAS = $90,000

Calculations
- 75% x FAS
- .75 x 90,000 = $67,500
- Annuity value of ASF = $4,137 ($50,000/12.086)
- <u>Estimated</u> annuity value of ITHP-NYC benefit = $2,500
- Annual pension benefit = $74,137 ($67,500 + 4,137 + 2,500)

Federal tax
- Annuity value of ASF = $4,137
- Estimated annual pension subject to federal tax = $4,137
- Annual pension not subject to federal tax = $70,000

Example #2 is a basic calculation of a retiring ADR member (using the same dollar figures as example 1) who has elected to take the full final withdrawal.

Assumptions
- 10-year ADR
- Retirement age = 41
- Required amount = $15,000
- ASF balance = $50,000
- Final withdrawal = Yes
- FAS = $90,000

Calculations
- 75% x FAS
- .75 x 90,000 = $67,500
- Annuity value of ASF = $4,137 ($50,000/12.086)
- <u>Estimated</u> annuity value of ITHP-NYC benefit = $2,500
- Annual pension benefit before final withdrawal = $74,137 ($67,500 + 4,137 + 2,500)
- Annuity value of final withdrawal = $4,013 ($48,500/12.086)
- Annual pension benefit after final withdrawal = $70,124 ($74,137 − 4,013)

Federal tax
- Annuity value of 10 % required amount = $124
- Estimated annual pension subject to federal tax = $124
- Annual pension not subject to federal tax = $70,000

Example #3 is a calculation of a retiring ADR member who has elected to not take a final withdrawal.

Assumptions
- 25-year ADR
- Retirement age = 48
- Required amount = $130,000
- ASF balance = $200,000
- Final withdrawal = No
- Earnings from 20-25 years = $550,000
- FAS = $120,000

Calculations
- 75% x FAS
- .75 x 120,000 = $90,000
- Value of 1/60ths = $9,166 ($550,000/60)
- Annuity value of ASF = $18,024 ($200,000/11.096)
- <u>Estimated</u> annuity value of ITHP-NYC benefit = $13,500
- <u>Estimated</u> annuity value of ITHP-NYC benefit over 20 = $3,600
- Annual pension benefit = $134,290
  ($90,000 + $9,166 + 18,024 + 13,500 + 3,600)

Federal tax
- Value of 1/60ths = $9,166
- Annuity value of ASF = $18,024
- <u>Estimated</u> value of ITHP-NYC benefit over 20 = $3,600
- Estimated annual pension subject to federal tax = $30,790
  ($9,166 + 18,024 + 3,600)
- Annual pension not subject to federal tax = $103,500

Chapter 1: NYPD Pension Tier 2

Example #4 is a calculation of a retiring ADR member (using the same dollar figures as example 3) who has elected to take the full final withdrawal.

Assumptions
- 25-year ADR
- Retirement age = 48
- Required amount = $130,000
- ASF balance = $200,000
- Final withdrawal = Yes
- Earnings from 20-25 years = $550,000
- FAS = $120,000

Calculations
- 75% x FAS
- .75 x 120,000 = $90,000
- Value of 1/60ths = $9,166 ($550,000/60)
- Annuity value of ASF = $18,024 ($200,000/11.096)
- <u>Estimated</u> annuity value of ITHP-NYC benefit = $13,500
- <u>Estimated</u> annuity value of ITHP-NYC benefit over 20 = $3,600
- Annual pension benefit before final withdrawal = $134,290 ($90,000 + 9,166 + 18,024 + 13,500 + 3,600)
- Annuity value of final withdrawal = $16,853 ($187,000/11.096)
- Annual pension benefit after final withdrawal = $117,437 ($134,290 − 16,853)

Federal tax
- Value of 1/60ths = $9,166
- Annuity value of 10 % required amount = $1,171
- <u>Estimated</u> value of ITHP-NYC benefit over 20 = $3,600
- <u>Estimated</u> annual pension subject to federal tax = $13,937 ($9,166 + 1,171 + 3,600)
- Annual pension not subject to federal tax = $103,500

Accidental Disability Retirement Pension Final Withdrawal vs. No Final Withdrawal

NYCPPF members receiving an ADR pension will have to decide whether to elect a final withdrawal or not. The concept is basically the same as the Service retiree: rollover to defer taxation, appreciation of the rollover account, ownership of funds, etc. There may be significant tax and retirement planning strategies available for the individual who receives an ADR pension and elects the final withdrawal.

Ordinary Disability Retirement Pension

The Ordinary Disability Retirement (ODR) pension is granted to a retiree who suffers an illness or injury that is not considered line of duty. A NYCPPF member who retires with an ODR does not receive the annual VSF payment and does not receive any VSF DROP payment, if applicable. In addition, an ODR pension is taxed by the federal government and possibly by state governments.

The basic annual ODR pension benefit is calculated as follows.

20 or more years of service
- $1/40^{th}$ for every year of service x FAS
- Plus, annuity value of the excess over the required amount <u>or</u> less the annuity value of a shortage

More than 10, but less than 20 years of service
- 50% of FAS
- Plus, annuity value of the excess over the required amount or less the annuity value of a shortage

Less than 10 years of service
- 33 1/3% of FAS
- Plus, annuity value of the excess over the required amount or less the annuity value of a shortage

Ordinary Disability Pension Calculations

> Example #1 is a basic calculation of a retiring ODR member who has elected not to take a final withdrawal.
>
> **Assumptions**
> - 22-year ODR
> - Retirement age = 44
> - Required amount = $90,000
> - ASF balance = $125,000
> - Excess = $35,000
> - Final withdrawal = No
> - FAS = $110,000
>
> **Calculation**
> - 1/40ths x years of service x FAS
> - .025 x 22 x 110,000 = $60,500
> - Annuity value of excess = $2,996 ($35,000/11.682)
> - Annual pension benefit = $63,496

Example #2 is a basic calculation of a retiring ODR member who has elected to take the full final withdrawal.

Assumptions
- 22-year ODR
- Retirement age = 44
- Required amount = $90,000
- ASF balance = $125,000
- Excess = $35,000
- Final withdrawal = Yes
- FAS = $110,000

Calculation
- 1/40ths x years of service x FAS
- .025 x 22 x 110,000 = $60,500
- Annuity value of excess = $2,996
- (35,000/11.682)
- Annual pension benefit before final withdrawal = $63,496
- Annuity value of final withdrawal = $9,929 ($116,000/11.682)
- Annual pension benefit after final withdrawal = $53,567 ($63,496 − 9,929)

Summary Table: Service, Accidental Disability, and Ordinary Disability Pension Benefits

TABLE #23			
Summary: Service vs. ADR, vs. ODR			
Item	Service	ADR	ODR
Annual VSF	Yes	No	No
VSF DROP	Yes	No (in most cases)	No
60ths benefit	Yes	Yes	No
ITHP-NYC benefit	Yes	Yes	No
Federal tax	Yes	Yes & No	Yes
NYS tax	No	No	No

Pension Options

A pension option is an election by the retired member to provide all or a portion of their pension benefit to someone else upon their death. The decision of whether to select a pension option is a difficult decision for some NYCPPF retirees. Generally, the decision is made at finalization and is irrevocable (in most cases). It should be noted that in some cases, the pre-retiree may be forced to select an option due to a divorce agreement. Finalization occurs when the NYC Chief Actuary can determine the final pension amount and the costs of the various options. As many are aware, the cost of a pension option is expensive for retired NYCPPF members. The reason the cost is so significant is the NYCPPF Board has not updated the option cost factors since 1985. As of the writing of this book, the NYCPPF Board is analyzing updated mortality tables and will hopefully approve the use of the new tables when determining pension option costs. In the author's opinion, if the option costs are updated more retiring members will consider a pension option for their beneficiary. Another significant issue regarding the costs of a pension option is generally the retiring NYCPPF member is currently not provided the cost during the retirement process. Clearly, this makes it extremely difficult for the retiring member to make an informed decision regarding the final withdrawal and other important retirement decisions.

Deciding to elect an option is based on many factors: personal choice, insurability, overall health, option cost, etc. ADR retirees should carefully analyze the selection of an option due to the favorable tax treatment available to a spouse beneficiary. The following are some advantages and disadvantages of selecting a pension option.

Advantages
- Medical evaluation is not required
- Retiree will know how much the pension will be for life and the life of the spouse/beneficiary
- No fees or commissions
- Spouse/beneficiary will not have to make investment decisions or go out into the marketplace to purchase an annuity
- COLA to the spouse

Disadvantages
- A younger retiree may be able to purchase life insurance at less cost than a pension option
- Survivorship pension is generally taxed as ordinary income at the federal level and possibly the state level
- Depending how long the retiree lives, the pension becomes eroded due to inflation (future value of money)

The following provides a brief summary of the available options.
- No option (maximum retirement allowance)
  - pension ends upon death of retiree
  - beneficiary receives nothing
- Option 2 (100% Joint & Survivor)
  - retiree receives reduced annual pension benefit
  - beneficiary receives 100% of reduced annual pension benefit
  - one beneficiary and cannot be changed
- Option 3 (50% Joint & Survivor)
  - retiree receives reduced annual pension benefit
  - beneficiary receives 50% of reduced annual pension benefit
  - one beneficiary and cannot be changed
- Option 4 (Lump Sum)
  - retiree receives reduced annual pension benefit

- retiree elects a lump sum amount for beneficiary
  - more than one beneficiary can be designated and can be changed
- Option 4 (Annuity)
  - retiree receives reduced annual pension benefit
  - retiree elects an annuity amount for beneficiary
  - one beneficiary and cannot be changed
- Option 5 (5 Year Certain)
  - retiree receives reduced annual pension benefit
  - if retiree dies before five years from retirement date, beneficiary receives pension until the fifth anniversary of retiree's retirement date
- Option 6 (10 Year Certain)
  - retiree receives reduced annual pension benefit
  - if retiree dies before ten years from retirement date, beneficiary receives pension until the tenth anniversary of retiree's retirement date

Note: There is also a "pop-up" feature offered with options 2, 3, & 4. The pop-up feature, if elected, allows the retiree's annual pension benefit to revert to the maximum retirement allowance if the beneficiary predeceases the retiree.

Pension Option Examples - Using 1985 Basis

Table #24 is an example of Option #3 (50% to the beneficiary) based on a 50-year-old Service retiree and a 48-year-old beneficiary.

Assumptions
- Maximum annual service pension = $120,000
- Required amount = $135,000
- ASF balance = $350,000 (all before-tax)
- Excess = $215,000
- Full final withdrawal available = $336,500
- Amounts listed are before-tax

TABLE #24
1985 Basis Option #3 (50% to Beneficiary)-Service Retiree

Item	No Withdrawal	Excess Only Withdrawal	Full Final Withdrawal
Annual pension (no option)	$120,000	$101,387	$90,868
Monthly pension (no option)	$10,000	$8,449	$7,572
Option cost (annual)	$10,056	$8,496	$7,615
Option cost (monthly)	$838	$708	$635
Annual pension to retiree	$109,944	$92,891	$83,254
Monthly pension to retiree	$9,162	$7,741	$6,938
Annual pension to beneficiary	$54,972	$46,445	$41,627
Monthly pension to beneficiary	$4,581	$3,870	$3,469

Table #25 is an example of Option #3 (50% to the beneficiary) based on a 50-year-old ADR retiree and a 48-year-old beneficiary. As indicated in the table, the option costs for an ADR retiree are more expensive than a Service retiree.

Assumptions
- Maximum annual ADR pension = $120,000
- Required amount = $135,000
- ASF balance = $350,000 (all before-tax)
- Excess = $215,000
- Full final withdrawal available = $336,500
- Amounts listed are before-tax

TABLE #25
1985 Basis Option #3 (50% to Beneficiary)-ADR Retiree

Item	No Withdrawal	Excess Only Withdrawal	Full Final Withdrawal
Annual pension (no option)	$120,000	$100,059	$88,790
Monthly pension (no option)	$10,000	$8,338	$7,399
Option cost (annual)	$14,100	$11,757	$10,433
Option cost (monthly)	$1,175	$980	$869
Annual pension to retiree	$105,900	$88,302	$78,357
Monthly pension to retiree	$8,825	$7,358	$6,530
Annual pension to beneficiary	$52,950	$44,151	$39,178
Monthly pension to beneficiary	$4,412	$3,679	$3,264

Table #26 is an example of Option #4.2 (100% to the beneficiary with a pop-up) based on a 50-year-old Service retiree and a 48-year-old beneficiary.

Assumptions
- Maximum annual service pension = $120,000
- Required amount = $135,000
- ASF balance = $350,000 (all before-tax)
- Excess = $215,000
- Full final withdrawal available = $336,500
- Amounts listed are before-tax

TABLE #26
1985 Basis Option #4.2 (100% to Beneficiary with Pop-up)-Service Retiree

Item	No Withdrawal	Excess Only Withdrawal	Full Final Withdrawal
Annual pension (no option)	$120,000	$101,387	$90,868
Monthly pension (no option)	$10,000	$8,449	$7,572
Option cost (annual)	$19,932	$16,841	$15,093
Option cost (monthly)	$1,661	$1,403	$1,258
Annual pension to retiree	$100,068	$84,546	$75,775
Monthly pension to retiree	$8,339	$7,045	$6,314
Annual pension to beneficiary	$100,068	$84,546	$75,775
Monthly pension to beneficiary	$8,339	$7,045	$6,314
Annual pension to retiree if beneficiary pre-deceases	$120,000	$101,387	$90,868
Monthly pension to retiree if beneficiary pre-deceases	$10,000	$8,449	$7,572

Pension Option Example - Using More Up-to-Date Mortality Tables

If the pension option costs are updated, the actual calculation of the maximum pension benefit will change. Basically, a NYCPPF member with an appointment date prior to the effective date of the change will have their pension calculated under two methods (in some cases three methods). The first method would be based on 1985 Basis, while the second method would be based on the new mortality tables. The retiring member will receive a pension based on the greater of the two (or three) methods. The following is an example of a pension option cost using up-to-date mortality tables. For simplicity, we will assume the maximum pension was based on 1985 Basis. Table #27 summarizes the results.

Chapter 1: NYPD Pension Tier 2

Assumptions
- 50-year-old Service retiree & 50-year-old beneficiary
- Maximum annual service pension = $85,000
- Required amount = $135,000
- ASF balance = $350,000 (all before-tax)
- Excess = $215,000
- Full final withdrawal available = $336,500
- Amounts listed are before-tax

TABLE #27

Option #3 (50% to Beneficiary)-Service Retiree

Item	No Withdrawal	Excess Only Withdrawal	Full Final Withdrawal
Annual pension (no option)	$85,000	$66,387	$55,868
Monthly pension (no option)	$7,083	$5,532	$4,656
Option cost (annual)	$3,196	$2,496	$2,102
Option cost (monthly)	$266	$208	$175
Annual pension to retiree	$81,804	$63,891	$53,766
Monthly pension to retiree	$6,817	$5,324	$4,480
Annual pension to beneficiary	$40,902	$33,193	$27,934
Monthly pension to beneficiary	$3,408	$2,766	$2,328

Table #28 compares the costs of a pension option using 1985 Basis vs. up-to-date mortality tables. The option costs are based on a 50-year old Service retiree, 50-year old beneficiary, and an annual pension of $85,000.

TABLE #28		
Pension Option Costs- 1985 Basis vs. Up-to-Date Mortality Tables		
Item	100% to Beneficiary	50% to Beneficiary
1985 Basis	$12,597	$6,800
Up-to-Date Tables	$6,162	$3,196
% Reduction	51%	53%

Cost of Living Adjustment

As previously reviewed, the Cost of Living Adjustment (COLA) for NYCPPF Tier 2 retirees is not very valuable. Members are entitled to COLA under the following conditions.

- Age 62 and retired for Service at least five years OR
- At age 55 and retired for Service at least ten years OR
- ADR or ODR retirees after being retired for five years, regardless of age
- A surviving spouse of an eligible retiree receiving a lifetime benefit (the spouse receives an increase equal to one-half the COLA the retiree would have received)

Eligible COLA retirees will receive 50% of the Consumer Price Index (CPI), with a minimum amount of 1% and a maximum of 3%. The COLA is only applied to the first $18,000 of the pension. Therefore, the minimum COLA is $180 per year and the maximum is $540 per year. Some retirees will receive a COLA on their pension, but the amount will be deducted from their annual VSF payment until age 62. After age 62, the retiree will no longer have the COLA amount deducted from the annual VSF benefit.

Pre-Retirement NYCPPF Tier 2 Steps

The following steps are provided as a general overview to assist NYCPPF Tier 2 pre-retirees with their retirement decisions.

1. Perform estimated pension benefit calculations based on different assumptions.
2. Determine optimal date to retire based on pension benefit, FAS, age, etc.
3. Determine if permissible service credits (buy-backs) are available.

Chapter 1: NYPD Pension Tier 2

4. If granted an ADR, understand the calculation of the pension and the tax implications.
5. Review different pension options (no option/max pension, 100%, 50%, etc.) and the costs.
6. Determine the amount of pension contributions/interest (final withdrawal) that are permitted to be removed at retirement.
7. Determine "cost" of final withdrawal.
8. Determine if after-tax contributions were made.
9. Determine if VSF DROP funds are available.
10. Review age 50 rule exception.
11. Research available governmental retirement plans available to accept rollovers.
12. Review tax and distribution rules of IRAs and all governmental retirement plans that are available.
13. Perform trustee-to-trustee rollovers.
14. If after-tax contributions were not removed, determine recovery method.
15. Collect pension benefit for many years.

Summary

Retiring from the NYPD is a difficult decision and should be based on an individual's personal situation. Before retiring, the NYPD member should fully understand both the advantages and disadvantages of retiring after 20 years of service vs. remaining on the job. Of course, retiring after 20 years would be ideal, but for many may not be realistic.

This chapter reviewed how the NYCPPF Tier 2 pension is calculated under various scenarios. The calculation of the NYCPPF Tier 2 pension is based on many factors: contribution rate, required amount, age at appointment, age at retirement, final average salary, years of service, value of ASF, type of retirement, etc.

Before retiring, every NYPD member should take the time to fully understand the pension, analyze their own situation, and project the value of the pension under different scenarios. After this analysis is done, the pre-retiree will be able to make a more informed and educated decision.

NYCPPF Tier 2 members contemplating retirement at 20 years, may want to review Case Study #3 in the Case Studies chapter.

CHAPTER 2
NYPD Pension Tier 3

New York City Police Pension Fund (NYCPPF) members hired after June 30, 2009 are in Tier 3. Tier 3 was created in 1976 but was never used by the NYCPPF. Prior to 2009, the Governor of New York would sign legislation extending the pension benefits of Tier 2 for new hires. During the recession of 2008, Governor David Patterson decided to not sign the extender bill which then forced new NYPD hires to be placed into Tier 3. Currently, Tier 3 consists of three plans; Original, Revised, and Enhanced. The differences between Tier 2 and Tier 3 are significant and it is important for Tier 3 members to educate themselves regarding how their own pension plan works. With Tier 3, the vast number of pension choices can be overwhelming and will require the member to have more than a basic understanding of the pension plan.

The Tier 3 pension is a defined benefit pension and is funded by NYCPPF members and NYC. The Tier 3 pension will be a critical funding mechanism for the member's retirement spending needs and in many cases may be the retirees most valuable retirement asset.

Generally, the NYCPPF Tier 3 pension plan is most favorable if the member completes 25 years of service. Working for the NYPD beyond 25 years of service provides no additional pension benefit except if the member can increase their final average salary (FAS) used in the pension calculation. NYCPPF Tier 3 members have a mandatory retirement age of 62, while Tier 2 members have a mandatory retirement age 63. The Social Security Offset (SSO) and the five-year average for some members are unfavorable aspects of Tier 3. A favorable component of Tier 3 is the escalation provision and should not be overlooked when making retirement decisions.

Note: This chapter is an overview of Tier 3 pension benefits and is subject to revision. Tier 3 members should be guided by NYCPPF personnel and documents.

Appointment Dates & Tier 3 Plans

Tier 3-Original
NYCPPF members with an appointment date between July 1st, 2009 and March 30th, 2012 are in Tier 3-Original, unless the member elected to opt-in to Tier 3-Enhanced.

Tier 3-Revised
NYCPPF members with an appointment date between April 1st, 2012 and March 30th, 2017 are in Tier 3-Revised, unless the member elected to opt-in to Tier 3-Enhanced.

Tier 3-Enhanced
NYCPPF members with an appointment date of on or after April 1st, 2017 are in Tier 3-Enhanced. Tier 3-Enhanced also includes Tier 3 Original & Revised members if they opted-in.

Pension Plan Contributions
NYCPPF Tier 3 members are not assigned a specific pension contribution rate based on their age at appointment. Tier 3 members are required to contribute a percentage of pensionable earnings (base salary, overtime, night differential, etc.) based on their Tier 3 plan. Table #29 displays the current NYCPPF member contribution rates.

TABLE #29

Tier 3 Pension Member Contribution Rates	
Plan	Rate
Original	3%
Revised	3%
Enhanced	4%

The Enhanced pension plan contributions can increase based on an analysis conducted by the NYC Actuary. The analysis will be done every three years and the rate can be increased to a maximum of 6% (3% base + 3% adjustment) for Enhanced members. Tier 3 Original and Revised member contribution rates are currently not subject to any increase.

The NYCPPF member contributions for Tier 3 members are not used to "purchase" an annuity through the NYCPPF. The contributions are simply used to fund the NYCPPF which ultimately provides the member's pension benefit. Pension plan contributions made by Tier 3 members earn a 5% fixed rate of interest and the interest is not relevant if a member has more than 10 years of service. The 5% interest rate would benefit a member who decides to leave or is fired from the NYPD prior to the completion of 10 years. If a member has less than 10 years of service, the pension contributions can be removed from the NYCPPF. If a member has more than 10 years of service, the pension contributions cannot be removed from the NYCPPF.

The City of New York does not provide an employer pick-up (ITHP) for Tier 3 members, members are not permitted to contribute additional money to the NYCPPF, and contributions are required for 25 years. Tier 3 members are also not permitted to opt-out of contributing to the NYCPPF; they must contribute their required rate. Additionally, Tier 3 members are currently <u>not</u> permitted to take a pension loan.

Taxation of Pension Plan Contributions

All the pension contributions made by Tier 3 members are contributed on a pre-tax basis <u>except</u> for Original and Revised members who opted-in to the Enhanced plan. Members who opted-in to the Enhanced plan have pre-tax basic contributions and post-tax contributions on the additional (currently 1%) contributions.

Final Average Salary

Final Average Salary (FAS) is the starting point in calculating a Tier 3 pension. The FAS a retiring member can use is based on their Tier 3 plan and the type of retirement (Service vs. Disability). The average earnings used in the FAS calculation for all Tier 3 members are limited to 10% based on a certain number of prior years.

FAS Tier 3-Original

For FAS, these members will use the greater of three consecutive calendar years or the final 36 months if they are entitled to a Service or Vested retirement. If the member opted into Tier 3-Enhanced and retires with a Disability retirement, the FAS is based on the greater of five consecutive calendar years or final 60 months.

FAS Tier 3-Revised & Enhanced

These members are only entitled to use the greater of five consecutive calendar years or the final 60 months whether they receive a Vested, Service, or Disability retirement. Exception: Tier 3 Original members who opted-in to the Enhanced plan can still use the more favorable three year or 36-month FAS calculation if they retire for Service or Vest.

FAS-Three Consecutive Calendar Years

Table #30 is an example of the three consecutive calendar years calculation for FAS without the pensionable earnings being limited. Table #31 is an example of the pensionable earnings being limited. In order to correctly calculate the three consecutive calendar years, the member needs to account for the two previous calendar years and use 10% as a limit.

TABLE #30			
FAS- Three Consecutive Years 10% Rule			
Year	Pensionable Earnings	Earnings Limit	Pensionable Earnings for FAS
1	$142,000	$154,000	$142,000
2	$138,000	$140,250	$138,000
3	$130,000	$134,750	$130,000
4	$125,000	N/A	N/A
5	$120,000	N/A	N/A
Three Year Average = $136,667			

TABLE #31			
FAS- Three Consecutive Years 10% Rule			
Year	Pensionable Earnings	Earnings Limit	Pensionable Earnings for FAS
1	$155,000	$156,750	$155,000
2	$148,000	$145,750	$145,750
3	$137,000	$136,400	$136,400
4	$128,000	N/A	N/A
5	$120,000	N/A	N/A
Three Year Average = $145,717			

FAS-Five Consecutive Calendar Years

Table #32 is an example of the five consecutive calendar years calculation for FAS with the pensionable earnings being limited. In order to correctly calculate the five consecutive calendar years, the member needs to account for the four previous calendar years and use 10% as a limit. The five-year FAS is extremely unfavorable since <u>nine</u> years are used in the calculation.

\multicolumn{4}{c}{TABLE #32}
\multicolumn{4}{c}{FAS- Five Consecutive Years 10% Rule}
Year	Pensionable Earnings	Earnings Limit	Pensionable Earnings for FAS
1	$160,000	$157,575	$157,575
2	$153,000	$150,425	$150,425
3	$146,000	$143,825	$143,825
4	$141,000	$139,425	$139,425
5	$133,000	$135,850	$133,000
6	$127,000	N/A	N/A
7	$122,000	N/A	N/A
8	$125,000	N/A	N/A
9	$120,000	N/A	N/A
\multicolumn{4}{c}{Five Year Average = $144,850}

Reviewing table #32 indicates a total of $8,750 of pensionable earnings was not used to determine the five-year FAS of $144,850. Comparing this five-year calculation with the three-year calculation (using the same pensionable earnings) results in a FAS of $153,000 for the three-year calculation. Based on a 50% Service pension, the five-year FAS member would receive a pension of $72,425 while the three-year FAS member would receive $76,500.

> **Author's Tip**
>
> For help with FAS average calculations use the Tax & RP App iPhone app. The app has four averaging calculators; 12 months 20% limit, 3-year average 10% limit, 3-year average 20% limit, and 5-year average 10% limit.

Social Security Offset

The Social Security Offset (SSO) is an unfavorable provision of Tier 3 and applies to all Tier 3 members except Tier 3 Enhanced members who retire with a Disability pension (Ordinary or Accidental). The dollar value of the SSO is determined when the member retires and is based on earnings for service with public employers in New York State. As an example, if the retiree previously worked for the State of New York prior to NYPD employment, the earnings from the state job will be used in addition to the NYPD earnings when calculating the SSO.

The SSO for a Service or Vested retirement begins at age 62. The SSO will apply even if the member is not receiving a Social Security Retirement benefit. If an Ordinary Disability retiree (except Tier 3 Enhanced) is eligible for Social Security Disability benefits before age 62, the SSO will apply. If an Accidental Disability retiree (except Tier 3 Enhanced) is also receiving a Social Security Disability benefit, the SSO begins immediately regardless of age.

Note: The author uses different estimates for the SSO in the Tier 3 pension calculation examples in this book. The reader's SSO may be higher or lower at retirement. It is difficult to project what a member's SSO offset will be in the future due to how the Social Security Administration calculates the benefit. For example, the Social Security Administration uses "bend points", index factors, and indexed earnings when calculating the value of the benefit. Additionally, it is difficult to anticipate how Social Security benefits will be calculated in the future based on funding issues of the Social Security program.

Escalation

Escalation is an interesting and favorable feature of Tier 3 pensions. Escalation is an increase (or decrease) to the retired member's pension based on the Consumer Price Index (CPI). The largest percentage increase escalation can be in a year is 3%, while the lowest is negative 3%.

To be eligible for "full escalation", the Tier 3 Service Retirement member must complete 25 years of service or defer the Vested/Service pension to his or her 25th anniversary. Full escalation is also provided to Tier 3 Original & Revised members if they are granted an Ordinary Disability Retirement (ODR) pension or Accidental Disability Retirement (ADR) pension, regardless of the number of years of service. Tier 3 Enhanced members who are granted an ODR or ADR pension do not receive escalation but will receive the "regular" Cost of Living Adjustment (COLA), when eligible. Escalation is also provided to a beneficiary if the retiree selected a pension option during the retirement process.

Note: Escalation examples are based on NYCPPF's interpretation of how escalation is calculated. As per the NYCPPF's Tier 3 FAQs on their website, the SSO does not affect escalation:

"Escalation will be calculated annually based on the original retirement allowance (that has grown and compounded up to 3% in escalation annually) <u>before</u> the Social Security Offset is applied". The author uses an assumed escalation rate of 2.5%, the same assumption rate used by the NYC Actuary. Also, for Tier 3 pension calculation examples, the author has omitted any COLA increases if the member is not entitled to escalation. In the author's opinion, COLA is not significant enough since it is only based on the first $18,000 of the pension benefit.

Cost of Living Adjustment

As per the NYC Administrative Code, the retired member or beneficiary is entitled to the greater of escalation or the regular COLA. COLA is provided under the following conditions.

- Age 62 and retired for Service at least five years OR
- At age 55 and retired for Service at least ten years OR
- ADR or ODR retirees after being retired for five years, regardless of age
- A surviving spouse of an eligible retiree receiving a lifetime benefit (the spouse receives an increase equal to one-half the COLA the retiree would have received)

Eligible COLA retirees will receive 50% of the Consumer Price Index (CPI), with a minimum amount of 1% and a maximum of 3%. The COLA is only applied to the first $18,000 of the pension. Therefore, the minimum COLA is $180 per year and the maximum is $540 per year. Some retirees will receive a COLA on their pension, but the amount will be deducted from their annual VSF payment until age 62. After age 62, the retiree will no longer have the COLA amount deducted from the annual VSF benefit.

Pensions of Tier 3

Basically, there are four types of pensions in Tier 3 with many variations. In general, the variations are related to escalation. The four basic types are:

- Vested Retirement
- Early Service Retirement
- Normal Service Retirement
- Disability Retirement- Ordinary (ODR) & Accidental (ADR)

Vested Retirement

NYCPPF Tier 3 members are entitled to a Vested Retirement pension after five years of service. The vested member must wait until the 20th anniversary year to be eligible to collect the pension benefit. The Vested member has two choices at the 20th anniversary; begin to collect the pension or defer until 22 years and one month or more, up to the 25th anniversary, to be eligible for escalation. The following is the formula for a Vested pension if deferral is not elected:

- 2.1% x FAS x years of service
- Less 50% of Social Security Benefit (SSB) at age 62

As an example, assume a 35-year-old Tier 3-member vests after 10 years of service. The pension calculation is as follows:

- 2.1% x $100,000 x 10 = $21,000 annual pension
- Less 50% of SSB at age 62.

If the Vested member elects to collect the $21,000 after 10 years (20th anniversary) there is no escalation. The Vested member will receive a total pension amount of $357,000 (17 years x $21,000) before the SSO is applied.

Alternatively, the Vested member could elect to defer the pension to receive escalation. For example, assume a 35-year old Tier 3–member vests after 10 years of service, but elects to defer the pension for 15 years (25th anniversary). As a result of the deferral, the Vested pension benefit is calculated as follows.

- 2.0% x $100,000 x 10 = $20,000 annual pension
- Less 50% of SSB at age 62.

Since the member deferred the Vested pension, the percentage multiplied by FAS is reduced to 2.0% and escalation is applied to the $20,000 annual pension. If the Vested member elected to collect the $21,000 after 10 years (20th anniversary) there is no escalation.

Note: There is an eligibility to collect exception for the Tier 3 member who becomes 55 years old before the 20th anniversary. Review the NYCPPF Tier 3 Summary Plan Description for more information.

Early Service Retirement Pension

After the completion of 20 years of service, NYCPPF Tier 3 members are entitled to an Early Service Retirement pension. The Early Service Retirement pension is 42% (not 50%) of FAS if the member completes exactly 20 years. If the member completes exactly 21 years of service, the Early Service Retirement pension is 46% of FAS.

Table #33 displays the percentage multiplied by FAS based on months after the 20th anniversary.

The Early Service Retirement member has two choices at their retirement date; begin to collect the pension immediately or defer until 22 years and one month or more, up to the 25th anniversary, to be eligible for escalation. The following is the formula for an Early Service Retirement pension if deferral is not elected.

- 2.1% x FAS x years of service PLUS
- 1/3% of FAS for each month after 20 years
- Less 50% of SSB at age 62

As an example, assume a 45-year-old Tier 3-member retires after 20 years of service. The pension calculation is as follows.

- 2.1% x $125,000 x 20 = $52,500 annual pension
- Less 50% of SSB at age 62.

TABLE #33
Early Service Retirement-Percentages

Years/Months	Percentage
20/0	42%
20/1	42.33%
20/2	42.67%
20/3	43%
20/4	43.33%
20/5	43.67%
20/6	44%
20/7	44.33%
20/8	44.67%
20/9	45%
20/10	45.33%
20/11	45.67%
21 years	46%
21/1	46.33%
21/2	46.67%
21/3	47%
21/4	47.33%
21/5	47.67%
21/6	48%
21/7	48.33%
21/8	48.67%
21/9	49%
21/10	49.33%
21/11	49.67%
22 years	50%

If the Early Service Retirement member elects to collect the $52,500 at the 20th anniversary there is no escalation, but there is COLA when eligible. The Early Service Retirement member will receive a total pension amount of $892,500 (17 years x $52,500) plus COLA before the SSO is applied. Using an SSO amount of $12,000, the Early Service Retirement member's pension is reduced to approximately $40,500 plus COLA for the rest of his/her life. If the Early Service Retirement member lives to 85 years old, the total pension received is $1,824,000 plus COLA.

Alternatively, the Early Service Retirement member could elect to defer the pension to receive escalation. For example, assume a 45-year old Tier 3–member receives an Early Service Retirement after 20 years of service, but elects to defer the pension for five years (25th anniversary). As a result of the deferral, the pension benefit is calculated as follows:

- 2.0% x $125,000 x 20 =$50,000 annual pension
- Less 50% of SSB at age 62.

Due to the deferral, the percentage multiplied by FAS gets lowered from 2.1% to 2.0%. Since the member deferred the pension, escalation is applied to the $50,000 annual pension. The full escalation rate will apply on the $50,000 annual pension benefit from 22 to 25 years even though the Early Service Retirement member is not receiving the pension benefit. The Early Service Retirement member who deferred will collect a total pension amount of approximately $761,385 (using an assumed 2.5% escalation rate) before the SSO is applied. At age 62, the value of the pension is approximately $72,415. Using an SSO amount of $12,000, the Early Service Retirement member's pension is reduced to $60,415 the first year of the SSO. If the Early Service Retirement member lives to 85 years old, the total pension received is $2,267,433.

Table #34 compares the two Early Service Retirement examples; no escalation and receive pension immediately vs. defer pension to get escalation.

TABLE #34
Early Service Retirement-Immediate/no Escalation vs. Deferred/Escalation

Age	Immediate/No	Deferred/Yes
45 to 50	$262,500	$0
50 to 62	$630,000	$761,385
62 to 85	$931,500	$1,506,048
Total Pension Received	$1,824,000	$2,267,433

The Early Service Retirement pension with the five-year deferral to be eligible for escalation may be advantageous for the member who is going to get another full-time job after 20 years of service with the NYPD. It should be noted that health insurance benefits are only provided to a retiree collecting a pension. Therefore, an individual who defers the pension is currently <u>not</u> eligible for health insurance during the deferral period.

Normal Service Retirement

After the completion of 22 years of service, NYCPPF Tier 3 members are entitled to a Normal Service Retirement pension. The following is the formula for a Normal Service Retirement pension.

- 50% x FAS
- Less 50% of SSB at age 62

As an example, assume a 50-year-old Tier 3-member retires after 22 years of service. The pension calculation is as follows.

- 50% x $130,000 = $65,000 annual pension
- Less 50% of SSB at age 62.

If the Normal Service Retirement member elects to collect the $65,000 at the 22nd anniversary there is no escalation, but there is COLA when eligible. The Normal Service Retirement member will receive a total pension amount of $780,000 (12 years x $65,000) plus COLA when eligible before the SSO is applied. Using an SSO amount of $13,200, the Normal Service Retirement member's pension is reduced to $51,800 plus COLA for the rest of his or her life. If the Normal Service Retirement member lives to 85 years old, the total pension received is $1,971,400 plus COLA.

Alternatively, the Tier 3 Normal Service Retirement member can elect to defer the pension to receive escalation. For example, assume a 50-year old Tier 3–member receives a Normal Service Retirement after 22 years of service, but elects to defer the pension for three years (25th anniversary). As a result of the deferral, the pension benefit is calculated as follows:

- 50% x $130,000 = $65,000 annual pension
- Less 50% of SSB at age 62

Unlike the Early Service Retirement, there is no reduction of the percentage (50%) multiplied by FAS if a Normal Service Retirement member elects to defer the pension. Since the member deferred the pension, escalation is applied to the $65,000 annual pension. The full escalation rate will apply on the $65,000 annual pension benefit from 22 to 25 years even though the Normal Service Retirement member is not receiving the pension benefit. After the three-year deferral period, the Normal Service Retirement member will begin to collect the pension benefit which has appreciated to $69,998. The Normal Service Retirement member who deferred will receive a total pension amount of approximately $714,215 (using an assumed 2.5% escalation rate) before the SSO is applied. At age 62, the value of the pension is approximately $87,418. Using an SSO amount of $13,200, the Normal Service Retirement member's pension is reduced to $74,218 the first year of the SSO. If the Normal Service Retirement member lives to 85 years old, the total pension received is $3,084,238.

Finally, if a Tier 3 Normal Service Retirement member has more than 22 years of service but less than 25 years of service, they are entitled to partial escalation. The partial escalation is 1/36th of the full escalation rate for each month after the 22nd year anniversary. Table #35 displays the factors that can be used in determining the partial escalation.

TABLE #35

Partial Escalation Factors

Years/months	Factor	Years/Months	Factor	Years/Months	Factor
22/1	.0277	23/1	.3601	24/1	.6925
22/2	.0554	23/2	.3878	24/2	.7202
22/3	.0831	23/3	.4155	24/3	.7479
22/4	.1108	23/4	.4432	24/4	.7756
22/5	.1385	23/5	.4709	24/5	.8033
22/6	.1662	23/6	.4986	24/6	.8310
22/7	.1939	23/7	.5263	24/7	.8587
22/8	.2216	23/8	.5540	24/8	.8864
22/9	.2493	23/9	.5817	24/9	.9141
22/10	.2770	23/10	.6094	24/10	.9418
22/11	.3047	23/11	.6371	24/11	.9695
23 years	.3324	24 years	.6648	25 years	1.000

To use table #35, simply locate the years/months that you will have worked beyond 22 years of service. To the right of the years/months is the factor to be used when calculating partial escalation. For example, assume a retiring Normal Service Retirement member will have completed 23 years and 10 months at retirement. Using the table, the partial escalation factor is .6094. The partial escalation factor is then multiplied by the escalation rate every year to determine how much of the escalation the retired member is entitled to.

Normal Service Retirement-25 Years of Service

If a NYCPPF Tier 3 Normal Service Retirement completes 25 years of service, full escalation will apply the first day of the following month. The pension calculation is the same as the Normal Service Retirement.

Chapter 2: NYPD Pension Tier 3

- 50% x FAS
- Less 50% of SSB at age 62

As an example, assume a 50-year-old Tier 3 Normal Service Retirement member retires after 25 years of service. The pension calculation is as follows.

- 50% x $130,000 = $65,000 annual pension
- Less 50% of SSB at age 62

The Normal Service Retirement member is eligible for full escalation the first day of the month after retirement on the pension of $65,000. The Normal Service Retirement member will receive a total pension amount of approximately $919,129 (using an assumed 2.5% escalation rate) before the SSO is applied. At age 62, the value of the pension is approximately $87,418. Using an SSO amount of $15,000, the Normal Service Retirement member's pension is reduced to $72,418 the first year of the SSO. If the Normal Service Retirement member lives to 85 years old, the total pension received is $3,247,751.

Tier 3 Breakeven Analysis

If you enjoy working with numbers and spreadsheets, calculating Tier 3 breakeven points can almost be endless. The Tier 3 pension has so many different combinations that can be used in calculating the pension benefit; immediate, defer, escalation, partial escalation, years and months of service, SSO, etc. Due to the difficulty in calculating the value of the SSO, the member performing a breakeven analysis will have to estimate the amount.

Tier 3 Breakeven Analysis Examples

Example #1 is a breakeven analysis, table #36 displays the results, based on a Normal Service Retirement scenario using different years of service.

- 45-year-old with 23 years of service vs.
- 47-year-old with 25 years of service

Assumptions (45-year-old)
- FAS = $150,000
- Annual pension = $75,000
- No deferral
- 2.5% assumed escalation rate during entire escalation period
- Eligible for partial escalation (2.5% x .3324 = .00831)
- SSB calculated based on 23 years of service
- SSO = $13,800

Assumptions (47-year-old)
- FAS = $155,000
- Annual pension = $77,500
- 2.5% assumed escalation rate during entire escalation period
- Eligible for full escalation
- SSB calculated based on 25 years of service
- SSO = $15,000

TABLE #36		
Breakeven Analysis-23 Years vs. 25 Years		
Age	45-Year-Old Adjusted Annual Pension	47-Year-Old Adjusted Annual Pension
45	$75,623	$0
46	$76,252	$0
47	$76,885	$79,438
48	$77,524	$81,423
49	$78,168	$83,459
50	$78,818	$85,545
51	$79,473	$87,684
52	$80,133	$89,876
53	$80,799	$92,123
54	$81,471	$94,426
55	$82,148	$96,787

Chapter 2: NYPD Pension Tier 3

Age	45-Year-Old Adjusted Annual Pension	47-Year-Old Adjusted Annual Pension
56	$82,830	$99,207
57	$83,519	$101,687
58	$84,213	$104,229
59	$84,913	$106,835
60	$85,618	$109,505
Total	**$1,288,389**	**$1,312,224**
61	$86,330	$112,243
Total	**$1,374,718**	**$1,424,467**
62	$72,530	$100,049
63	$73,247	$102,925
64	$73,971	$105,874
65	$74,700	$108,895
66	$75,435	$111,993
67	$76,177	$115,168
68	$76,925	$118,422
69	$77,679	$121,757
70	$78,439	$125,176
71	$79,205	$128,681
72	$79,978	$132,273
73	$80,757	$135,955
74	$81,543	$139,728
Total	**$2,375,303**	**$2,971,363**
75	$82,335	$143,597
76	$83,134	$147,561
77	$83,940	$151,626
78	$84,752	$155,791
79	$85,571	$160,061
80	$86,397	$164,437
81	$87,229	$168,923
82	$88,069	$173,521
83	$88,916	$178,235
84	$89,769	$183,065
Total	**$3,235,416**	**$4,598,181**

Reviewing table #36 indicates that the 47-year-old who completed 25 years of service begins to surpass the 45-year-old who completed 23 years of service at approximately 60 years old. At 62 years old, the 25 years of service retiree is ahead by approximately $50,000 and at 75 years old is ahead by approximately $596,000.

Example #2 is a breakeven analysis, table #37 displays the results, based on a Normal Service Retirement scenario using different years of service and older retirement ages.

- 55-year-old with 23 years of service vs.
- 57-year-old with 25 years of service

Assumptions (55-year-old)
- FAS = $150,000
- Annual pension = $75,000
- No deferral
- 2.5% assumed escalation rate during entire escalation period
- Eligible for partial escalation (2.5% x .3324 = .00831)
- SSB calculated based on 23 years of service
- SSO = $13,800

Assumptions (57-year-old)
- FAS = $155,000
- Annual pension = $77,500
- 2.5% assumed escalation rate during entire escalation period
- Eligible for full escalation
- SSB calculated based on 25 years of service
- SSO = $15,000

Chapter 2: NYPD Pension Tier 3

TABLE #37
Breakeven Analysis-23 Years vs. 25 Years & 55 & 57 Years Old

Age	55-Year-Old Adjusted Annual Pension	57-Year-Old Adjusted Annual Pension
55	$75,000	N/A
56	$75,623	N/A
57	$76,252	$77,500
58	$76,885	$79,438
59	$77,524	$81,423
60	$78,168	$83,459
61	$78,818	$85,545
62	$65,673	$72,684
63	$66,333	$74,876
64	$66,999	$77,123
65	$67,671	$79,426
66	$68,348	$81,787
67	$69,030	$84,207
68	$69,719	$86,687
69	$70,413	$89,229
70	$71,113	$91,835
Total	**$1,277,770**	**$1,280,219**
71	$71,818	$94,505
72	$72,530	$100,049
73	$73,247	$102,925
74	$73,971	$105,874
75	$74,700	$108,895
76	$75,435	$111,993
77	$76,177	$115,168
78	$76,925	$118,422
79	$77,679	$121,757
Total	**$1,830,524**	**$2,134,991**
80	$78,439	$125,176
81	$79,205	$128,681

Age	55-Year-Old Adjusted Annual Pension	57-Year-Old Adjusted Annual Pension
82	$79,978	$132,273
83	$80,757	$135,955
84	$81,543	$139,728
Total	**$2,230,447**	**$2,796,804**

Reviewing table #37 indicates that the 57-year-old (25 years of service) retiree begins to surpass the 55-year-old (23 years of service) retiree at approximately 70 years old. At 71 years old, the 57-year-old (25 years of service) retiree is ahead by approximately $2,500 and at 80 years old is ahead by approximately $304,467.

Example #3 is a breakeven analysis, table #38 displays the results, based on a Normal Service Retirement scenario using different years of service and older retirement ages.

- 55-year-old with 25 years of service vs.
- 60-year-old with 30 years of service

Assumptions (55-year-old)
- FAS = $150,000
- Annual pension = $75,000
- 2.5% assumed escalation rate during entire escalation period
- Eligible for full escalation
- SSB calculated based on 25 years of service
- SSO = $15,000

Assumptions (60-year-old)
- FAS = $165,600
- Annual pension = $82,800
- 2.5% assumed escalation rate during entire escalation period
- Eligible for full escalation
- SSB calculated based on 30 years of service
- SSO = $18,000

TABLE #38
Breakeven Analysis-25 Years vs. 30 Years (55 & 60 years old)

Age	55-Year-Old Adjusted Annual Pension	60-Year-Old Adjusted Annual Pension
55	$76,875	N/A
56	$78,797	N/A
57	$80,767	N/A
58	$82,786	N/A
59	$84,856	N/A
60	**$86,977**	**$84,870**
61	$89,151	$86,992
62	$74,151	$68,992
63	$76,380	$71,167
64	$78,665	$73,396
65	$81,006	$75,681
66	$83,406	$78,023
67	$85,867	$80,423
68	$88,388	$82,884
69	$90,973	$85,406
70	$93,622	$87,991
71	$96,338	$90,641
72	$99,121	$93,357
73	$101,974	$96,141
74	$104,899	$98,994
75	$107,896	$101,919
76	$110,969	$104,917
77	$114,118	$107,990
78	$117,346	$111,140
79	$120,654	$114,368
80	$124,046	$117,677
81	$127,522	$121,069
82	$131,085	$124,546
83	$134,737	$128,110
84	$138,481	$131,763
Total	**$2,961,854**	**$2,418,455**

Reviewing table #38 indicates that the 55-year old's (25 years of service) adjusted annual pension is already larger than the 60-year old's (30 years of service) annual pension when he/she begins to collect. Further reviewing table #36 indicates that the 55-year-old (25 years of service) has his/her pension reduced to $74,151 the first year of SSO while the 60-year-old (30 years of service) has his/her pension reduced to $68,992 the first year of SSO. Even at age 85, the 55-year-old (25 years of service) would have received more pension income (+$543,399) than the 60-year-old (30 years of service) at 85 years old. Although not displayed in the table, the 55-year-old (25 years of service) would still have received more pension income (+$623,974) than the 60-year-old (30 years of service) at 95 years old.

Tier 2 vs. Tier 3 Analysis

Many people often state that Tier 3 is an inferior pension plan when compared to Tier 2. Is that an accurate statement? The best way to find out is to go through an example.

Assumptions (Tier 2 50-year old)
- 25 years of service
- FAS = $150,000
- Value of 60ths = $11,600
- Estimated annuity value of ITHP-NYC benefit = $3,600
- Member's ASF balance = $300,000
- Required amount = $70,000
- Excess = $230,000
- No final withdrawal
- Annual pension = $110,115
- COLA, when eligible = $225 per year

Assumptions (Tier 3 50-year old)
- 25 years of service
- FAS = $150,000
- Annual pension = $75,000
- 2.5% assumed escalation rate during entire escalation period
- Eligible for full escalation
- SSB calculated based on 25 years of service
- SSO = $15,000

Chapter 2: NYPD Pension Tier 3

TABLE #39		
Tier 2 vs. Tier 3		
Age	*Tier 2 Adjusted Annual Pension*	*Tier 3 Adjusted Annual Pension*
50	$110,115	$76,875
51	$110,115	$78,797
52	$110,115	$80,767
53	$110,115	$82,786
54	$110,115	$84,856
55	$110,115	$86,977
56	$110,115	$89,151
57	$110,115	$91,380
58	$110,115	$93,665
59	$110,115	$96,006
60	$110,340	$98,406
61	$110,340	$100,867
Total	**$1,321,830**	**$1,060,533**
62	$110,340	$85,867
63	$110,340	$88,388
64	$110,340	$90,973
65	$110,340	$93,622
66	$110,340	$96,338
67	$110,340	$99,121
68	$110,340	$101,974
69	$110,340	$104,899
70	$110,340	$107,896
71	$110,340	$110,969
72	$110,340	$114,118
73	$110,340	$117,346
74	$110,340	$120,654
Total	**$2,756,250**	**$2,392,699**
75	$110,340	$124,046
76	$110,340	$127,522

Age	Tier 2 Adjusted Annual Pension	Tier 3 Adjusted Annual Pension
77	$110,340	$131,085
78	$110,340	$134,737
79	$110,340	$138,481
80	$110,340	$142,318
81	$110,340	$146,251
82	$110,340	$150,282
83	$110,340	$154,414
84	$110,340	$158,649
Total	**$3,859,650**	**$3,800,482**

As indicated in table #39, the Tier 2 retiree received significantly more total pension than the Tier 3 retiree at age 62 and at age 75. At age 85, the Tier 2 retiree has received about 1% more than the Tier 3 retiree. At approximately age 87, the Tier 3 pension becomes more favorable than Tier 2.

This analysis was based on the Tier 2 member having a significant excess ($230,000) in their ASF account. If the excess was only $100,000, the Tier 3 retiree begins to receive more total pension than the Tier 2 retiree at approximately 78 years old.

Variable Supplement Fund

Very simply, if a NYCPPF Tier 3 member retires (Early Service Retirement) with 20 years of service or more they will receive the annual Variable Supplement Fund (VSF) payment. Currently, the annual VSF payment is $12,000 and is distributed to Service retirees only; Ordinary and Accidental retirees do not receive the annual VSF benefit. The annual VSF payment is taxed by the federal government, but not taxed by NYS/NYC.

VSF Deferred Retirement Option Plan

The Variable Supplement Fund Deferred Retirement Option Plan (VSF DROP) became effective on January 1st, 2002. The VSF DROP, also referred to as banked VSF, is beneficial to the NYCPPF member who decides to stay on the job past 20 years of service. Prior to 2002, the member who decided to remain on the job after 20 years of service forfeited the annual VSF payment. Now, once 20 years of service is reached and the member does not retire, the VSF begins to get "banked." For some Tier 3 members there is an exception to the banked VSF after

Chapter 2: NYPD Pension Tier 3

20 years of service. If a Tier 3 member defers the Early or Normal Service Retirement pension, the VSF is currently <u>not</u> banked.

Upon retirement, the NYCPPF member will need to decide what to do with the VSF DROP money, if applicable. Basically, there are two choices; roll it over or distribute it. For most, the best choice would be to rollover the funds in order to avoid immediate taxation and a penalty, if applicable. Table #40 displays the tax and penalty consequences of the VSF DROP.

TABLE #40
VSF DROP Taxable & 10% Penalty

	IRS Age	Taxable	10% Penalty
Not rolling over VSF DROP	Less than 50	Yes	Yes
Not rolling over VSF DROP	50 and over	Yes	No
Rolling over VSF DROP	Any age	No	No
Distributions from new retirement plan	N/A	Yes	Yes, if less than 59 ½ years old (exceptions)

VSF DROP money can be rolled over to the following:

- Individual Retirement Account (IRA)
- Roth Individual Retirement Account (Roth IRA)
- NYC Deferred Compensation Plan Pension Rollover Account "Special 401(k)"
- Union Annuity Plan (in some cases)
- New employer retirement plan

Once the VSF DROP money is rolled over to the new retirement plan it will be subject to the distribution rules of the new retirement plan. For example, assume a 51-year-old NYCPPF Tier 3 member retires and rolls over the VSF DROP to an IRA and the following year takes a distribution from the IRA. In this case, the member would be subject to the 10% early distribution penalty unless an exception applies. Prior to rolling over the VSF DROP funds, the pre-retiree should be familiar with the "age 50 rule" exception.

Accidental Disability Retirement Pension

The Accidental Disability Retirement (ADR) pension is based on Tier 3 plans. Tier 3 Original & Revised members are entitled to escalation. The calculation for ADR is as follows.

- 50% of FAS
- Less 50% of Social Security Disability Benefit at age 62 or earlier

The following is an example of a Tier 3 Original member who receives an ADR pension and is <u>not</u> eligible for Social Security Disability benefits.

Assumptions
- 15 years of service
- 45 years old at retirement
- FAS = $130,000
- 2.5% assumed escalation rate during entire escalation period
- Eligible for full escalation
- SSB calculated based on 15 years of service
- SSO = $9,000

Calculation
- 50% x $130,000 = $65,000
- Less 50% of SSB at age 62

The Tier 3 Original ADR member will receive a total pension amount of approximately $1,390,113 (using an assumed 2.5% escalation rate) before the SSO is applied. At age 62, the value of the pension is approximately $98,905. Using an SSO amount of $9,000, the ADR member's pension is reduced to $89,905 the first year of the SSO.

Tier 3 Enhanced ADR members are <u>not</u> entitled to escalation but will receive COLA when eligible. There is <u>no</u> SSO for Tier 3 Enhanced ADR members. The calculation for ADR Enhanced is as follows.

- 75% of FAS

The following is an example of a Tier 3 Enhanced member who receives an ADR pension.

Assumptions
- 15 years of service
- 45 years old at retirement
- FAS = $130,000
- COLA, when eligible

Calculation
- 75% x $130,000 = $97,500

The Tier 3 Enhanced ADR member will receive a total pension amount of $487,500 before COLA eligibility. After five years of retirement, the ADR member will receive COLA. The ADR pension will only increase incrementally throughout the member's lifetime due to COLA.

Ordinary Disability Retirement Pension

An Ordinary Disability Retirement (ODR) pension is granted to a Tier 3 member if they are also eligible to receive a Social Security Disability Benefit. The member must have at least five years of service and not be eligible for a Normal Service Retirement. The ODR pension is also based on Tier 3 plans. Tier 3 Original & Revised members are entitled to escalation. The calculation for ODR is as follows.

- 33 1/3% of FAS OR
- 2% of FAS x years of service
- Less 50% of Social Security Disability Benefit

The following is an example of a Tier 3 Original member who is eligible for a Social Security Disability benefit and receives an ODR pension.

Assumptions
- 15 years of service
- 45 years old at retirement
- FAS = $120,000
- 2.5% assumed escalation rate during entire escalation period
- Eligible for full escalation
- SSB calculated based on 15 years of service
- SSO = $9,000

Calculation
- 33 1/3% x $120,000 = $40,000 OR
- 2% x $120,000 x 15 = $36,000
- Less SSO

The Tier 3 Original ODR member's pension of $40,000 will be eligible for escalation but will be immediately reduced due to the SSO.

Tier 3 Enhanced ODR members are not entitled to escalation but will receive COLA when eligible. There is no SSO for Tier 3 Enhanced ODR members. The calculation for ODR Enhanced is as follows.

- 33 1/3% of FAS <u>OR</u>
- 2% of FAS x years of service

The following is an example of a Tier 3 Enhanced member who receives an ODR pension.

Assumptions
- 15 years of service
- 45 years old at retirement
- FAS = $120,000
- COLA, when eligible

Calculation
- 33 1/3% x $120,000 = $40,000 <u>OR</u>
- 2% x $120,000 x 15 = $36,000

The Tier 3 Enhanced ODR member's pension of $40,000 will <u>not</u> be eligible for escalation, but COLA will apply after five years of retirement. There is <u>no</u> SSO for Tier 3 Enhanced ODR.

Pension Options

The pension options offered to Tier 3 members are <u>not</u> the same as Tier 2 members. A pension option is an election by the retiring member to provide all or a portion of their pension benefit to someone else upon their death. As per the NYCPPF's Tier 3 SPD, retiring Tier 3 members will be provided the costs of the pension options at retirement. Tier 3 retired members generally must choose an option or no option within 30 days of retirement.

The following are some advantages and disadvantages of selecting a pension option.

Advantages
- Medical evaluation is not required
- Retiree will know how much the pension will be for life and the life of the spouse/beneficiary

- No fees or commissions
- Spouse/beneficiary will not have to make investment decisions or go out into the marketplace to purchase an annuity
- Escalation or COLA to the spouse

Disadvantages
- A younger retiree may be able to purchase life insurance at significantly less cost than a pension option
- Survivorship pension is generally taxed as ordinary income at the federal level and possibly the state level
- Depending how long the retiree lives, the pension becomes eroded due to inflation (future value of money)

The following provides a brief summary of the available options for Tier 3.
- No option (maximum retirement allowance)
  - pension ends upon death of retiree
  - beneficiary receives nothing
- Option 1 (100% Joint & Survivor)
  - retiree receives reduced annual pension benefit
  - beneficiary receives 100% of reduced annual pension benefit
  - one beneficiary and cannot be changed
- Option 2 (Annuity)
  - retiree receives reduced annual pension benefit
  - retiree elects an annuity amount from 10% to 90% for beneficiary
  - one beneficiary and cannot be changed
- Option 3 (5 Year Certain)
  - retiree receives reduced annual pension benefit
  - if retiree dies before five years from retirement date, beneficiary receives pension until the 5th anniversary of retiree's retirement date
  - after the five-year period, the beneficiary does not receive anything
- Option 4 (10 Year Certain)
  - retiree receives reduced annual pension benefit

- if retiree dies before 10 years from retirement date, beneficiary receives pension until the 10th anniversary of retiree's retirement date
- after the ten-year period, the beneficiary does not receive anything
- Option 5A (50% Joint and Survivor with "Pop-up")
  - retiree receives reduced annual pension benefit
  - beneficiary receives 50% of reduced annual pension benefit
  - if the beneficiary predeceases the retiree, the pension reverts (pops-up) to the maximum pension
  - one beneficiary and cannot be changed
- Option 5B (100% Joint and Survivor with "Pop-up")
  - retiree receives reduced annual pension benefit
  - beneficiary receives 100% of reduced annual pension benefit
  - if the beneficiary predeceases the retiree, the pension reverts (pops-up) to the maximum pension
  - one beneficiary and cannot be changed

Summary

This chapter reviewed the different types of pensions for NYCPPF Tier 3 members. Tier 3 members should educate themselves regarding the different intricacies of their specific pension plan. Tier 3 can be confusing based on the different plans; Original, Revised, and Enhanced.

There are some unfavorable components to Tier 3; five-year average FAS calculation, no increased pension benefit beyond 25 years of service, SSO offset, etc. A very favorable component is escalation. Escalation should be thoroughly understood when making Tier 3 retirement decisions.

CHAPTER 3
NYPD Pension & Divorce

Divorcing and divorced NYPD members often have significant retirement planning challenges that are very different from non-divorced NYPD members. If an ex-spouse (alternate payee) is entitled to a portion of the member's pension, the decision of when to retire may become even more difficult. The process of separating the pension and other retirement plans (NYCDCP, IRAs, etc.) can be confusing, overwhelming, depressing, and expensive. When going through a divorce both the employee spouse and the non-employee spouse will need to educate themselves regarding the steps of the divorce process, tax issues, and at a minimum the basic concepts of retirement plans and pensions. Readers of this chapter should be aware that every divorce case is different and the services of a knowledgeable lawyer and a financial professional familiar with retirement plans and the pension may be worth the expense. The importance of a financial professional should not be overlooked since many lawyers may not be familiar with the intricacies of the pension, NYCDCP, Union Annuity Plan, etc.

Certified Divorce Financial Analyst®

A Certified Divorce Financial Analyst® (CDFA®) is a professional who comes from a financial planning, accounting or legal background and goes through an intensive training program to become skilled in analyzing and providing expertise related to the financial issues of divorce.

A CDFA® professional knowledgeable about pensions, the NYCDCP, and tax issues can provide valuable insight into the separation of the various retirement assets.

A CDFA® professional can be retained to become part of the divorce team providing litigation support for the lawyer and client. Occasionally, CDFA® professionals are also retained for collaborative divorces. In a collaborative divorce, both parties hire their own lawyer and sign an agreement to resolve the divorce without resorting to litigation.

Majauskas Formula

During a divorce, individuals need to become familiar with various terms. One of these terms is the "Majauskas formula". The Majauskas formula was established by the NY State Court of Appeals in Majauskas v. Majauskas and is most commonly used for the equitable distribution of a public pension. The "standard" formula (also referred to as the coverture fraction) is as follows.

- 50% × years of service credit accrued during marriage (numerator) divided by total service credit at time of retirement (denominator)

For example, a NYCPPF member has 22 years of service while married and has 25 years of total service at retirement and the two parties have agreed to split the marital portion by 50%. First, calculate the coverture fraction.

- 50% x 22/25 = 44%

At retirement, the NYCPPF member's pension will be 56% and the ex-spouse will receive 44%. If the NYCPPF member's pension is $70,000 per year; the NYCPPF member will receive $39,200 ($70,000 x 56%) per year and the ex-spouse will receive $30,800 ($70,000 x 44%) per year.

There are other equitable distribution choices besides the "standard" Majauskas formula that the two divorcing parties can agree to use.

- Negotiate the factors of the Majauskas equation
- Freeze the ex-spouse's share of the pension to the salary and service levels in place at the time of the commencement date of the divorce action
- A flat dollar amount or fixed percentage

Shared-Interest

The previous example, using the Majauskas formula, is an example of a shared-interest pension benefit. Very simply, the ex-spouse shares the pension benefit of the NYCPPF member which was calculated based on the member's actuarial factors. Generally, the ex-spouse must wait until the NYCPPF member retires before he or she will receive a pension benefit. Under a separate-interest pension benefit, the ex-spouse's portion is "carved-out" and can be provided to the ex-spouse even though the employee has not retired. The NYCPPF only divides pension benefits using the shared-interest approach.

Domestic Relations Order

A Domestic Relations Order (DRO) is a court order (legal document) that grants a person a right to a portion of the NYCPPF pension benefit his or her former spouse has earned through participating in the NYCPPF. Basically, an approved DRO tells the NYCPPF how to divide the pension benefit. The NYCPPF will divide the pension benefit as directed in the approved/certified DRO; a NYCPPF pension benefit cannot be divided without an approved/certified DRO.

There are many intricacies of preparing a DRO regarding the NYCPPF pension benefit and are not reviewed in this book. Both the employee/retired NYCPPF member and the alternate payee (ex-spouse) should fully understand the DRO before submitting it to the court for final approval/certification.

Note: Many people refer to the DRO as a QDRO (pronounced as KWAH dro). Technically, the NYCPPF will not accept a qualified DRO since it is a governmental plan and is not subject to the Employee Retirement Income Security Act of 1974 (ERISA). Instead of the term "qualified", NYCPPF uses the term "approved" DRO.

Pension Valuation-Pension Offset

At some point during the divorce process, a NYCPPF pension valuation may need to be performed. The pension valuation should be performed by a financial professional who has some experience with the pension system; the NYCPPF does not perform pension valuations for divorcing members.

A pension valuation is a calculation performed to determine the lump sum present value of a stream of pension payments. After the present value is determined, the marital portion of the pension can be calculated based on certain factors. In general, a pension valuation is useful if the pension is going to be offset with other assets.

The following is a <u>basic</u> example of a pension valuation being used to offset the NYCPPF pension benefit with other assets.

Assumptions
- NYPD member age = 45
- Pension benefit at cut-off date = $5,000 per month
- Discount rate = 3.2%
- Mortality table = RP-2000
- Coverture fraction = 46.87
- Value of jointly owned marital home = $500,000 (no mortgage)
- NYCDCP (NYPD member) marital account balance = $400,000

Results
- Present value of NYCPPF pension = $1,280,118
- NYPD member's portion = $680,127
- Alternate payee's portion = $599,991

Table #41 displays the results of an equitable division of the assets based on the NYPD member keeping the entire NYCPPF pension benefit.

TABLE #41

Pension Offset		
Item	NYPD Member	Other Party
NYPD Pension	$599,991	$0
Marital home	$0	$500,000
NYCDCP	$150,000	$250,000
Total	**$749,991**	**$750,000**

Summary

For divorced NYPD members, this chapter provided a brief overview regarding the division of the pension benefit due to a divorce. In many cases, retirement decisions for a divorced NYPD member are vastly different than a non-divorced NYPD member. Divorcing and divorced NYPD members need to carefully review the Domestic Relations Order in reference to the pension.

CHAPTER 4
NYC Deferred Compensation Plan

History

The New York City Deferred Compensation Plan (NYCDCP) was established in 1986 and consisted of only the 457(b) plan. The plan was first offered to NYC managers and then expanded to include NYC uniformed members (Police, Fire, etc.) and then ultimately civilian members. The total number of members participating in 1986 was approximately 4,500.

From 1986 to 1993, the plan offered four investment choices.

- Money Market/Savings Account
- Guaranteed Investment Contract (GIC)/Stable Income Fund
- Equity Index Fund (Vanguard Index Fund)
- Socially Responsible Fund (Dreyfus Third Century Fund)

In 1994, the NYCDCP made significant changes to their investment choices for participants by offering a total of eight options.

- Savings Account
- Stable Income Fund
- Long Term Bond Fund (Vanguard Fixed Income Securities Fund Long-Term US Treasury Portfolio)
- Balanced Fund (Chancellor Capital Management Fund)
- Socially Responsible Fund (Neuberger & Berman Management, Inc.)
- Equity Index Fund (Vanguard Institutional S&P 500 Index Fund)

- International Equity Fund (Morgan Stanley Institutional Active Country Allocation Portfolio)
- Small Cap Equity Fund (AIM Constellation Fund)

It is interesting to note that in 1994, the Socially Responsible Fund was structured as a separately managed account. In later years, the NYCDCP eventually changed other investment options to separately managed accounts. A potential advantage of a separately managed account is a lower asset management fee. A disadvantage may be the limited amount of research material available.

In the early years of the plan many NYC employees were hesitant to join due to the overall structure of the plan. A major disadvantage of the early plan was that the contributions made by employees were considered assets of NYC. This disadvantage was eventually corrected in December 1998 by having the employee contributions directed to a custodial account for the exclusive benefit of the employee. Another disadvantage of the early plan was that NYS taxes were owed upon distribution to a non-resident. Prior to 1996, distributions from the NYCDCP were subject to NYS taxes regardless of where the participant resided. The State Taxation of Pension Income Act of 1995 corrected this taxation whereby a distribution would no longer be subject to NYS taxes for a non-resident. Another disadvantage for the first fifteen years of the plan was that separated (retired) participants were required to select the month and year when distributions would occur within sixty days following separation of service. In 2002, the sixty-day distribution election was no longer required, which allowed retirees greater flexibility in determining when to receive distributions from their plan.

In 1997, the NYCDCP investment fund offerings were modified as follows.

- Money Market Fund (AIM Advisors, Inc.)
- Stable Income Fund
- Intermediate Term Bond Fund (Morgan Grenfell Fixed Income Fund)
- Balanced Fund (Vanguard Wellington Fund)
- Equity Index Fund (Vanguard Institutional Index Fund)
- Socially Responsible Fund (Neuberger & Berman NYC Deferred Comp Socially Responsible Trust)
- International Equity Fund (T. Rowe Price International Stock Fund)
- Small Cap Equity Fund (T. Rowe Price New Horizon Fund)

Chapter 4: NYC Deferred Compensation Plan

By the end of the year 2000, there were over 106,000 participants in the NYCDCP and had net assets available for plan participants of over $4.3 billion. The maximum yearly amount an individual could contribute to the plan was $8,000.

In 2001, significant changes occurred to the investment offerings of the NYCDCP. The Money Market Fund and the Balanced Fund were eliminated. A Mid Cap Fund and four Pre-Arranged Portfolios became available to participants. At the end of 2001, the investment offerings were as follows.

- Stable Income Fund
- Bond Fund (PIMCO Total Return Fund)
- Equity Index Fund (Vanguard Institutional Index Plus Fund)
- Socially Responsible Fund (separate account-Domini Social Investments)
- Mid Cap Equity Fund (Invesco Dynamics Fund)
- International Equity Fund (Capital Guardian International Equity Fund)
- Small Cap Equity Fund (T. Rowe Price New Horizons Fund)
- Pre-Arranged Portfolio A
- Pre-Arranged Portfolio B
- Pre-Arranged Portfolio C
- Pre-Arranged Portfolio D

In 2002, the NYCDCP began to offer another defined contribution retirement plan to its participants, the 401(k) plan. The 401(k)-plan offered the same investment choices as the 457(b) plan and permitted participants to contribute to both plans. Also, in 2002, the NYCDCP converted most of the investment offerings from mutual funds to separately managed accounts and an asset-based fee (.03%), in addition to the quarterly administrative fee, was implemented.

In 2004, the NYCDCP added a self-directed brokerage account option which permitted participants to transfer 20% of their account balance to an outside brokerage company. The self-directed brokerage account allows the participant to choose from thousands of mutual funds.

In 2005, the NYCDCP permitted participants to receive loans from the 457(b) plan and/or 401(k) plan. There are various rules and fees regarding NYCDCP loans, which will be reviewed later. Also, in 2005, the NYCDCP replaced the four Pre-Arranged Portfolios with nine Time-Based Portfolios (Pre-Arranged Portfolios).

During 2006, the NYCDCP began to offer four more retirement plans; the Roth 401(k), the New York City Employee (NYCE) IRA, NYCE Roth IRA, and the 401(a) Savings Incentive Plan.

In 2017, the NYCDCP started to allow participants to perform in-plan rollovers. An in-plan rollover permits a participant to convert pre-tax 457(b) funds to a Roth 457(b) or pre-tax 401(k) funds to a Roth 401(k). As a result of the American Taxpayer Relief Act of 2012, a separation of service is <u>not</u> required. In-plan rollovers may be advantageous for certain active NYPD members. In-plan rollovers will be reviewed in the Advanced Tax & Retirement Planning chapter.

Today, the NYCDCP offers the following retirement plans to its participants.

- 457(b)
- Roth 457(b)
- 401(k)
- Roth 401(k)
- 401(k) Pension Rollover Account ("Special" 401(k))
- 401(a) Savings Incentive Plan (currently only available to members of the LBA & CEA)
- NYCE IRA (employee and spouse)
- NYCE Roth IRA (employee and spouse)

The eight retirement plans offer the same investment choices.

- Stable Income Fund
- Bond Fund
- Equity Index Fund
- Global Socially Responsible Index Fund
- Mid-Cap Equity Index Fund
- International Equity Fund
- Small-Cap Equity Fund
- Pre-Arranged Portfolios (Static Allocation Fund and 2005 through 2055)

This brief history of the NYCDCP clearly shows that the plan has evolved into a unique, optional retirement plan for both active and retired NYPD members. The NYCDCP has been a popular and simple way for many NYPD members to fund their retirement goals and has resulted in the assets of the NYCDCP recently surpassing $21 billion.

Investment Funds

The eight retirement plans of the NYCDCP offer the same investment choices. Currently, there are seven (7) core funds offered.

- Stable Income Fund
- Bond Fund
- Equity Index Fund
- Socially Responsible Fund
- Mid-Cap Equity Fund
- International Equity Fund
- Small-Cap Equity Fund

In addition to the seven core funds, the NYCDCP also offers pre-arranged portfolios. The pre-arranged portfolios may be useful for the participant who would rather select a time period of when distribution of the account will occur. For example, if a participant anticipates retiring and starting distributions from their NYCDCP account in the year 2020, the 2020 Fund may be appropriate.

Besides the seven core funds and the pre-arranged portfolios, there is another investment choice in the NYCDCP. The self-directed option gives participants the ability to transfer up to 20% of their 457(b) or 401(k) balance to an outside brokerage account. Utilizing the self-directed option allows the participant to select investments from thousands of different types of mutual funds: micro-cap, real estate, natural resources, international bonds, emerging markets, etc. Investing in individual stocks, individual bonds, options, etc. is not permitted. Some NYPD members may find the self-directed option useful for the following reasons.

- Diversification. The current choice of funds in the NYCDCP may not provide true diversification for some participants. The financial markets consist of many different types of assets/investments not offered by the NYCDCP. As an example, all five of the NYC pension fund systems diversify across many different asset classes in order to reduce risk and attempt to maintain consistency of returns.
- This option allows the participant to add mutual funds of real estate, natural resources, micro-cap, international bond, emerging markets, dividend paying companies, and many others.

- Some plan participants may consider their account to be "over weighted" in the US equity funds (small cap, mid cap, and equity index) in the plan. Adding different asset classes may help to reduce the overall risk of the participants' account.

NYCDCP Fees

The fees charged to NYCDCP participants consist of three components: the quarterly administrative fee, the asset-based fee, and investment management fees. The quarterly administrative fee is straightforward and is charged to a participant at a current rate of $20 per quarter for a total of $80 per year. The fee is clearly listed on a participant's account statement on a quarterly basis. For participants who use the self-directed option, there is an additional $12.50 quarterly administrative fee. The quarterly administrative fees are a significant part of the overall revenue stream of the NYCDCP and is used to pay for salaries, administrative support, recordkeeping costs, etc. The asset-based fee is based on the net asset values of each of the seven core investment options and the Treasury Inflation Protected Securities (TIPS) fund used for the pre-arranged portfolios. Currently, the asset-based fee is .04% or 4 basis points and is also used for NYCDCP administrative expenses. This fee is not displayed on the participant's statements; although it is disclosed in the NYCDCP Annual Reports and other literature. The third fee is the investment management fee. Each of the core investment funds and the TIPS fund charge an investment management fee which reduces the overall return of each of the funds. This fee is used by the investment companies to operate each of the funds.

Comparing NYCDCP vs. a Retail IRA

When the NYCDCP first started it was a cost-effective retirement plan option for NYPD members. Today, it is still somewhat cost effective, but due to the competitiveness of the financial services industry and new financial products, a knowledgeable investor could have their own retail IRA with extremely low ongoing expenses. The following is an example of a $200,000 NYCDCP 457(b) allocated as 30% bond fund, 25% equity fund, 15% mid-cap fund, 15% international fund, and 15% small-cap fund, compared to a retail IRA using low cost index and exchange traded funds.

NYC DCP 457(b) 2017 fees
- $80 annual administrative fee
- $80 asset-based fee
- $251 investment management fee
Total fees=$411

Retail IRA fees
- $0 annual administrative fee
- $0 asset-based fee
- $240 investment management fee
Total fees=$240

Comparing the fees of the NYCDCP 2020 pre-arranged portfolio fund with the Vanguard Target Retirement 2020 Fund, the fees for the NYCDCP fund are 115% higher based on an account balance of $200,000.

NYC DCP 457(b) 2020 Fund 2017 fees:
- $80 annual administrative fee
- $80 asset-based fee
- $480 investment management fee
Total fees=$560

Vanguard Target Retirement 2020 Fund fees
- $0 annual administrative fee
- $0 asset-based fee
- $260 investment management fee
Total fees=$260

NYCDCP Loans
An active NYPD member is eligible to take a loan from certain NYCDCP retirement plans. Only the NYCDCP 457(b) and the NYCDCP 401(k) have loan provisions; loans are not permitted from the Roth 457(b), Roth 401(k), 401(a), NYCE IRA, or NYCE Roth IRA. The following are a few highlights regarding NYCDCP loans.

- Retired NYPD members are not permitted to take a NYCDCP loan
- Minimum loan is $2,500
- Maximum loan is 50% of the account value in NYCDCP 457(b) or NYCDCP 401(k) OR $50,000 reduced by any loan(s) from the NYCPPF
- A maximum of two loans can be outstanding
- Interest rate on a loan is the prime rate (published in the Wall Street Journal) plus 1%
- There is a $50 fee to process the loan and a quarterly maintenance fee of $8.75

NYCDCP Loan at Retirement

Retiring with an outstanding NYCDCP loan at retirement is similar when an NYPD member retires with an outstanding pension loan. If the NYCDCP loan is not paid back, the retiree will be subject to income tax and possibly a 10% penalty on the total outstanding loan balance.

NYCDCP Loan Offset vs. Deemed Distribution

NYCDCP participants that have an outstanding loan at retirement may want to become familiar with the confusing differences between a loan offset and a deemed distribution. In general, a loan offset is permitted to be rolled over to avoid taxation while a deemed distribution is not permitted to be rolled over. If a NYCDCP participant has an outstanding loan at retirement and would prefer to rollover the outstanding loan to avoid taxation, a loan offset form provided by the NYCDCP will have to be submitted.

The Tax Cuts & Jobs Act (TCJA), signed by President Trump in December of 2017, changed the amount of time to complete a rollover for certain taxpayers with an outstanding loan at retirement. Previously, the taxpayer only had 60 days to complete the rollover to avoid paying taxes and a 10% penalty (in some cases) on the value of the outstanding loan. As per TCJA, taxpayers now have until the due date of their tax return of the year after the plan loan was offset. Even better, if a taxpayer files an extension the amount of time is extended all the way to October 15th. For some retirees, there may be an available strategy to reduce the amount of taxes owed when electing a loan offset instead of the deemed distribution.

NYCDCP Distributions

The following are the methods of distribution offered by the NYCDCP.

Chapter 4: NYC Deferred Compensation Plan

- Full withdrawal (100% of account balance)
- Periodic installment payments
- One-time partial payment (either based on a percent or a specific dollar amount)
- One-time partial payment and remaining balance as periodic installment payments
- Direct rollover/transfer to another retirement plan, IRA, or Roth IRA

The 100% full withdrawal is straightforward, the NYCDCP participant has simply elected to withdraw the entire account balance as a lump sum. Depending on the dollar amount of the lump sum and the participant's overall tax situation, this may not be the optimal tax planning strategy.

The periodic installment payments method of distribution may be a suitable tax planning strategy for the NYCDCP participant who wants to spread out distributions over multiple tax years. The NYCDCP participant can choose monthly, quarterly, semi-annually, or annual installment payments.

The one-time partial payment occurs when a NYCDCP participant requests a portion of the account balance. For example, a participant has a $200,000 account balance and requests $30,000 as a one-time payment. The remaining $170,000 continues to stay in the plan.

The one-time partial payment and periodic installment payments occurs when a NYCDCP participant requests a portion of the account balance and then for the remaining balance requests the periodic installment payments method. For example, a participant has a $200,000 account balance and requests $30,000 as a one-time payment and then the remaining $170,000 distributed on an annual basis for 10 years.

NYCDCP 457(b)

The NYCDCP 457(b) is the more prevalent plan for NYPD members. Generally, the main feature of the NYCDCP 457(b) plan is that distributions from the plan are not subject to the 10% early distribution penalty upon separation of service (in-service distributions are generally not permitted, except for hardship withdrawal, low balance account, or over 70 ½ years old). Contributions to the NYCDCP 457(b) plan are made by <u>active</u> NYPD employees using pre-tax dollars. Retired, vested, terminated, former employees, etc. are not permitted to contribute to the NYDCP 457(b) plan. A significant advantage of the NYCDCP 457(b) plan is the separate treatment of contributions in reference to other retirement plans. This separate treatment gives the NYPD member an advantage over employees in the private sector. An NYPD employee could essentially contribute the maximum yearly contribution to both the NYCDCP 457(b) and the NYCDCP 401(k).

The money contributed to the NYCDCP 457(b) plan is not subject to Federal, NYS, or NYC taxes which reduces an employee's current gross income. The appreciations of the funds inside of the NYCDCP 457(b) plan are tax-deferred; taxes are owed upon distribution to the participant or beneficiary.

NYCDCP 457(b) Contributions

Many NYPD members have been contributing to the NYCDCP 457(b) plan for years and may have a substantial balance at retirement. The contribution rules are straightforward and the maximum amount that can be contributed each year may increase based on inflation. The NYCDCP participant selects a certain percentage (1% to as much as 75% of a paycheck) of their earnings that are deposited into their NYCDCP 457(b) account on a pre-tax basis. It is interesting to note that NYCPPF member contributions (required & ITHP) are deducted first before the NYCDCP contributions are deducted from bi-weekly pay. The following is an example of how contributions to the NYCDCP 457(b) plan are calculated when a participant also contributes to the NYCPPF.

- Annual salary of $100,000
- NYCPPF contribution rate of 7.5%
- Election of ITHP waiver
- NYCDCP 457(b) plan contribution rate of 5%

Calculation
- $100,000 x .075 = $7,500
- $7,500 contributed to the NYCPPF
- $100,000 - $7,500 = $92,500
- $92,500 x .05 = $4,625
- $4,625 contributed to the NYCDCP 457(b) plan
- Gross income reduced to $87,875

The limit for normal contributions for calendar year 2019 is $19,000 for participants less than age 50. Participants age 50 or older can contribute an additional $6,000 for a total of $25,000. The normal contributions and the additional "catch-up" for participants age 50 or older may be adjusted for cost of living adjustments annually in $500 increments.

NYCDCP 457(b) Three-year "Catch-up"

The NYCDCP 457(b) plan also allows some participants to utilize a three-year "catch-up" (also referred to as the "Deferral Acceleration for Retirement") contribution option. Some NYCDCP 457(b) participants may not be able to participate in the catch-up due to their maximum contributions in each of the years they were eligible participants in the plan. For NYPD employees considering the catch-up it may be beneficial to contact personnel at the NYCDCP regarding their eligibility and for assistance with implementing. The following are some highlights of the three year "catch up" provision.

- Can only be used once
- Can be utilized three consecutive years before normal retirement age
- Not permitted in the year designated as normal retirement age
- Up to twice the applicable annual contribution amount may be allowed
- Participants cannot do both the age 50 or older contribution and the three-year catch-up at the same time
- Contributions are a fixed dollar amount per paycheck, not a percentage
- Funds are invested in the same way as the participant's regular contributions
- May contribute the **lesser of** twice the annual limit ($38,000 in 2019) **or** the normal contribution limit plus the amount of the normal contribution limit not used in prior years

Eligibility and the calculation of the three-year catch-up can be complicated and should only be done after reviewing both the IRS rules and NYCDCP 457(b) plan literature. Table #42 should be used as a reference point to determine the amount of unused deferrals.

TABLE #42

Historical 457(b) Maximum Annual Contributions

Years	Maximum Annual Contribution
1986 through 1997	$7,500*
1998 through 2000	$8,000*
2001	$8,500*
2002	$11,000
2003	$12,000
2004	$13,000
2005	$14,000
2006	$15,000
2007	$15,500
2008	$15,500
2009	$16,500
2010	$16,500
2011	$16,500
2012	$17,000
2013	$17,500
2014	$17,500
2015	$18,000
2016	$18,000
2017	$18,000
2018	$18,500
2019	$19,000

*For years 1979 through 2001, the method to calculate unused deferrals can be very complicated and is not reviewed in this book.

Chapter 4: NYC Deferred Compensation Plan

The following is a basic example of an eligible NYCDCP participant who did not contribute to the NYCDCP 457(b) plan at all in prior years.

- Participant will be eligible for full retirement in the year 2022 at age 45
- Participant's normal retirement age is 45
- Participant can use the three-year catch-up provision in years 2019, 2020, and 2021
- Participant was eligible to join the 457(b) plan in 2002 but never did
- Participant is eligible to contribute twice the annual amount
- Assume the $19,000 maximum limit stays the same for years 2020 & 2021

To take full advantage of the three-year catch-up, the participant may contribute a total of $114,000 as shown in table #43.

TABLE #43
457(b) Three-year Catch-up

Year	Maximum Contribution Limit	Additional Three-year Catch-up	Total Contributions
2019	$19,000	$19,000	$38,000
2020	$19,000	$19,000	$38,000
2021	$19,000	$19,000	$38,000
Total			$114,000

Further analyzing the example based on the participant's annual salary of $100,000 and contributing 7.5% on a pre-tax basis to the NYCPPF results in the following.

- $100,000 x .075 = $7,500 contributed pre-tax to NYCPPF
- $92,500 - $19,000 maximum contribution limit to NYCDCP 457(b) = $73,000
- $73,000 - $19,000 additional three-year catch-up to NYCDCP 457(b) = $54,000
- Federal gross income reduced (current tax savings) from $100,000 to $54,000

To take advantage of the three-year catch-up, the NYCDCP participant will need to be eligible and be able to afford the additional deferrals.

NYCDCP 457(b) at Retirement

Years ago, the retiring NYPD member was required to select a distribution date for the funds inside of the NYCDCP 457(b) plan. Today, the retiring NYPD member does not need to select any distribution date and has great flexibility in when and how distributions are received.

A decision that does have to be made at retirement is whether the retiree wants to leave the funds in the NYCDCP 457(b) plan or transfer the account to another type of retirement plan. For the retiree 40 to 59 years old, this decision should be easy. Leaving the funds in the NYCDCP 457(b) plan allows the retiree to take full advantage of the no 10% early distribution penalty feature. If the retiree were to transfer the NYCDCP 457(b) plan to a new retirement plan, the distribution rules of the new plan would apply. For example, assume a 45-year-old recent NYPD retiree decided to transfer his NYCDCP 457(b) plan to an IRA. Once the funds were transferred to the IRA, the retiree would be subject to the 10% early distribution penalty (unless an exception applies) if distributions were received before 59 ½ years old.

At retirement, the retired NYPD member has a few choices regarding the NYCDCP 457(b).

- Leave the funds invested in the NYCDCP 457(b) plan
- Rollover to an IRA either at a bank, brokerage, or NYCE IRA
- Convert to a Roth IRA either at a bank, brokerage, or NYCE Roth IRA
- Distributions
  - subject to taxes

NYCDCP Roth 457(b)

The NYCDCP Roth 457(b) plan is similar to the regular NYCDCP 457(b) plan, except the account is funded with after-tax dollars. The appreciations of the funds inside of the NYCDCP Roth 457(b) plan are tax-deferred and distributions are non-taxable, after certain conditions are met. In order to receive non-taxable distributions from the NYCDCP Roth 457(b) plan, the account must have been established for five years and at the time of distributions the participant is more than 59 ½ years old.

The three-year catch-up provision (DAR) is available in the NYCDCP Roth 457(b) plan. Loans are not permitted from the NYCDCP Roth 457(b) plan.

NYC DCP Roth 457(b) Contributions

Essentially, NYCDCP Roth 457(b) plan participants have chosen to pay taxes on their contributions now instead of in their retirement years. This choice may be worthwhile for NYPD employees who have amassed significant assets in their pre-tax retirement accounts or for members who want to diversify their future tax obligations. The NYCDCP Roth 457(b) plan may also be an excellent choice for the NYPD employee who is unable to contribute to a Roth IRA due to earnings greater than the threshold amount. There are no income limit restrictions when contributing to the NYCDCP Roth 457(b) plan. For example, if an NYPD employee has a salary of $125,000 and her spouse earns $150,000, they would generally not be permitted to make an annual contribution to a Roth IRA. Although their combined income exceeds the income threshold for Roth IRA contributions; the NYPD employee could contribute the maximum to the NYCDCP Roth 457(b) plan. In addition to contributing the maximum to the NYCDCP Roth 457(b) plan, the NYPD employee could also contribute the maximum to the NYCDCP Roth 401(k) plan. For these two plans, NYCDCP Roth 457(b) and NYCDCP Roth 401(k), contributions are considered separate and do not have to be aggregated.

NYCDCP Roth 457(b) at Retirement

Most retired NYPD members should consider transferring the NYCDCP Roth 457(b) plan to a Roth IRA in order to receive more favorable distribution features. There may be a few retired NYPD members who should not transfer to a Roth IRA based on age, number of years the NYCDCP 457(b) has been established, and overall purpose of the funds in the plan.

Qualified distributions from the NYCDCP Roth 457(b) plan can be entirely non-taxable (federal, state, & city) after certain conditions are met. Generally, there are three conditions for non-taxable distributions.

- Separate (retire) from the NYPD
- At least 59 ½ years old
- At least five taxable years since the initial contribution

Non-qualified distributions from the NYCDCP Roth 457(b) plan occur when the participant fails to meet one of the three conditions. The NYCDCP 457(b) plan does not have the same distribution features of the Roth IRA. The NYCDCP 457(b) plan does not allow for just the basis (non-taxable portion) to be distributed first. The following is an example of a retired

NYPD member who has received a non-qualified distribution (entire account balance) from the NYCDCP Roth 457(b) plan.

> **Assumptions**
> - 50-year-old retired NYPD member
> - Contributed a total of $50,000 to the NYCDCP Roth 457(b) plan while working for the NYPD
> - Retired NYPD member's NYCDCP Roth 457(b) plan account has appreciated to $65,000
> - Retired NYPD member receives a full distribution of the entire $65,000
>
> **Income tax implications**
> - No 10% early withdrawal penalty even though the retiree is less than 59 ½ years old
> - Income tax owed on only $15,000; the original $50,000 is considered a return of basis and is not subject to income tax

One of the disadvantages of the NYCDCP Roth 457(b) plan is that the original contributions cannot be solely distributed without income tax consequences. In the previous example, if the NYPD retiree only needed a distribution of $50,000, the $50,000 would be part taxable ($11,500) and part non-taxable ($38,500). Although, there is a strategy available if the retiree only wanted to receive the $50,000 non-taxable funds.

NYCDCP Roth 457(b) and Isolation of Basis

As previously reviewed, the Roth 457(b) plan does not have the same rules as a Roth IRA regarding the isolation of non-taxable basis. A Roth IRA owner is permitted to remove the after-tax basis of contributions at any time, while generally the Roth 457(b) plan participant is not permitted to.

Currently, there are two tax planning strategies available for a Roth 457(b) plan participant to isolate the after-tax contributions made to the plan.

Chapter 4: NYC Deferred Compensation Plan

1. Roll over the Roth 457(b) account to a Roth IRA.
2. As per final regulations issued by the IRS in 2016, a Roth 457(b) participant could instruct the NYCDCP to direct the earnings portion of the Roth 457(b) plan to be rolled over to a Roth IRA and the after-tax contributions distributed to the participant.

Tax planning strategy #1 is easy to do. If a Roth 457(b) plan participant is eligible to take a distribution (distributable event), the participant simply instructs the NYCDCP to roll over the entire balance of the Roth 457(b) plan into a Roth IRA. Once the funds are in the Roth IRA, the Roth IRA owner would then be able to remove just the contributions (non-taxable portion). Tax planning strategy #2 is a little more involved and is <u>required</u> to be offered by a plan administrator (NYCDCP).

The following is an example of tax planning strategy #2 under the new rules. Assume a 50-year-old NYPD member has terminated employment (distributable event) and has a $50,000 Roth 457(b) plan balance, consisting of $35,000 contributions and $15,000 earnings. The individual has decided to take a total distribution of $50,000. The individual directs the NYCDCP to directly roll over the $15,000 into a Roth IRA. The result would be the following: The $15,000 directly rolled over to a Roth IRA would not be subject to current taxation/penalty, and the $35,000 paid to the participant would consist entirely of non-taxable money. Under the old rules, the $35,000 paid to the participant would consist of $24,500 of after-tax money and $10,500 of pre-tax/taxable money. The $15,000 directly rolled into the Roth IRA would consist of $10,500 of after-tax money and $4,500 of pre-tax/taxable money.

> **Author's Tip**
>
> Even though the separation of non-taxable basis is permitted in a Roth IRA, there are other factors to consider: age of the individual, five-year rule, penalty-free withdrawals, etc. In some cases, it may make sense to leave the funds in the Roth 457(b) plan.

NYCDCP Roth 457(b) and Required Minimum Distributions

If a retired member, who is approaching 70 ½ years old and still has a NYCDCP Roth 457(b) plan, the account should be rolled over to a Roth IRA. The NYCDCP Roth 457(b) plan requires distributions at 70 ½ years old while the Roth IRA does not.

NYCDCP 457(b) vs Roth 457(b) -Lower Paid NYPD Employee

Many lower-paid NYPD employees often choose to participate in the NYCDCP 457(b) plan. In most cases, these members should consider contributing to the NYCDCP Roth 457(b) plan due to their lower income tax bracket. As the NYPD employee earns more money and their income tax bracket increases, they should consider switching to the 457(b) plan. The earlier a younger and lower-paid NYPD employee contributes to the Roth 457(b) plan, more of the appreciation of the account can ultimately avoid taxation. For example, assume a 22-year-old NYPD employee contributes $15,000 over a five-year period into the NYCDCP Roth 457(b) plan. After the five years, the account has appreciated to approximately $16,577 based on a 5% rate of return and the employee stops contributing to the NYCDCP Roth 457(b) plan. At age 60, the NYCDCP Roth 457(b) value has grown to approximately $82,938 based on a 5% rate of return. The employee will avoid taxation on $67,938 ($82,938 - $15,000) of appreciation.

Summary Table of NYCDCP 457(b) vs. NYCDCP Roth 457(b)

TABLE #44		
457(b) vs. Roth 457(b)		
Item	*457(b)*	*Roth 457(b)*
Contributions reduce current taxable income	Yes	No
2019 Contribution Limits	$19,000 if less than 50 years old $25,000 if more than 50 years old $38,000 for three-year catch-up	
Contributions limited by gross income	No	No
Earnings/investment growth	Tax-deferred	Tax-deferred and then non-taxable if qualified
Federal tax on distributions	Taxable income	Non-taxable if distributions are qualified
10% Early Distribution Penalty	No	No

NYCDCP 401(k)

There are two significant differences between the NYCDCP 457(b) plan and the NYCDCP 401(k) plan; the 10% early distribution penalty and in-service distributions. The 10% early distribution penalty generally applies to distributions from the NYCDCP 401(k) plan prior to the age of 59 ½ years old (unless an exception applies). An important exception to the 10% penalty is the "age 50 rule". A participant 59 1/2 years old or older who has not retired from the NYPD could elect to receive distributions (in-service distribution) from the NYCDCP 401(k) plan. Active NYPD employees often fund the NYCDCP 401(k) plan after they have fully funded their annual NYCDCP 457(b) plan contribution.

NYCDCP 401(k) Contributions

NYCDCP 401(k) plan contributions are based on pre-tax earnings, account grows tax-deferred, and distributions are taxable. As stated earlier, distributions prior to 59 ½ years old are subject to the 10% early distribution penalty (unless an exception applies). If a NYPD employee can only afford to participate in one of the NYCDCP retirement plans, the NYCDCP 457(b) plan may be the better choice. Contributions to the NYCDCP 401(k) plan are treated as separate contributions from the NYCDCP 457(b) plan. Therefore, a NYPD employee could contribute the yearly maximum to both the NYCDCP 457(b) plan and the NYCDCP 401(k) plan.

NYCDCP 401(k) at Retirement

At retirement, the retired NYPD member has a few choices regarding the NYCDCP 401(k) plan.

- Leave the funds invested in the NYCDCP 401(k) plan
- Rollover to an IRA either at a bank, brokerage, or NYCE IRA
- Convert to a Roth IRA either at a bank, brokerage, or NYCE Roth IRA
- Distributions
  - subject to taxes and penalty, if applicable

NYCDCP Roth 401(k)

The NYCDCP Roth 401(k) plan is funded with after-tax dollars. The appreciation of the funds inside of the NYCDCP Roth 401(k) plan are tax-deferred and distributions can be non-taxable, after certain conditions are met. In order to receive non-taxable distributions from the Roth

401(k) plan, the account must have been established for five tax years and at the time of distributions the participant is more than 59 ½ years old.

NYCDCP Roth 401(k) Contributions

NYCDCP Roth 401(k) plan contributions are made with after-tax money, there are no income restrictions, and contributions are treated separately from the NYCDCP Roth 457(b) plan. If a NYPD employee can contribute to one of the NYCDCP Roth accounts, the NYCDCP Roth 457(b) plan may be the better choice.

NYCDCP Roth 401(k) at Retirement

The distribution features of the NYCDCP Roth 401(k) plan are similar to the NYCDCP Roth 457(b) plan. In most cases, the retired NYPD member should consider transferring the NYCDCP Roth 401(k) plan to a Roth IRA. At retirement, the retired NYPD member has a few choices regarding the NYCDCP Roth 401(k) plan.

- Leave the funds invested in the NYCDCP Roth 401(k) plan
- Rollover to a Roth IRA either at a bank, brokerage, or NYCE Roth IRA
- Distributions
    - subject to taxes and penalty, if applicable

NYCDCP Roth 401(k) and Required Minimum Distributions

If a retired member, who is approaching 70 ½ years old and still has a NYCDCP Roth 401(k), the account should be rolled over to a Roth IRA. The NYCDCP Roth 401(k) requires distributions at 70 ½ years old while the Roth IRA does not.

NYCDCP "Special" 401(k)

The NYCDCP offers a specific retirement plan that accepts rollovers from the NYCPPF (final withdrawal), VSF DROP, and Union Annuity Plans. The retirement plan is known as a "Special" 401(k) plan or pension rollover account. In general, the Special 401(k) plan has the same federal taxation distribution rules as the NYCDCP "regular" 401(k) plan. Although, there is a significant amount of confusion regarding the NYS taxation of this retirement plan. The short answer is that some (in most cases) of the money, when distributed to the retiree, is not subject to NYS/NYC income taxes. It is the responsibility of the taxpayer or tax preparer to calculate what portion is NYS/NYC taxable and what portion is non-taxable. The NYCDCP does <u>not</u> perform this calculation for participants. If you rolled over funds at retirement to the NYCDCP Special 401(k) plan it is critical to maintain documentation of the amounts rolled over, dates, etc.

NYCDCP 401(a)

The NYCDCP 401(a) plan, also known as the "Savings Incentive Plan", is currently only available to active members of the LBA & CEA. The NYCDCP 401(a) plan is entirely funded by NYC and participant contributions are not permitted. NYC may contribute (amount varies) to a participant's NYCDCP 401(a) plan if the participant contributes at least 1% of wages to the NYCDCP. Distributions from the NYCDCP 401(a) plan generally occur after separation of service and distributions prior to age 59 ½ are subject to the 10% early distribution penalty (unless an exception applies). A participant 62 years old or older who has not retired from the NYPD could elect to receive distributions (in-service distribution) from the NYCDCP 401(a) plan.

NYCDCP 401(a) at Retirement

At retirement, the retired NYPD member has a few choices regarding the NYCDCP 401(a) plan.

- Leave the funds invested in the NYCDCP 401(a) plan
- Rollover to an IRA either at a bank, brokerage, or NYCE IRA
- Convert to a Roth IRA either at a bank, brokerage, or NYCE Roth IRA
- Distributions
    - subject to taxes and penalty, if applicable

NYCE IRA

Most active NYPD employees do not contribute to the NYCE IRA for various reasons: maximizing NYCDCP 457(b) plan contributions, maximizing pension contributions, exceed income limits for deductibility, etc. The NYCE IRA may be suitable for a spouse of an NYPD member who desires his/her own IRA.

NYCE Roth IRA

The NYCE Roth IRA is funded with after-tax dollars. Many active NYPD employees do not contribute to the NYCE Roth IRA for some of the same reasons as the NYCE IRA: funds are being directed to the NYCDCP 457(b) plan, pension contributions, etc. The Roth IRA is an interesting retirement plan with some tremendous advantages; a later chapter will review it.

NYCDCP & NYCPPF Plan Contributions

A question that NYPD employees often ask is, in what order and based on affordability should contributions be made to either the NYCDCP or the NYCPPF? The following order of contributions may assist NYPD employees (Tier 2) in their decision-making process.

1. Regular/basic NYCPPF contributions (do not opt out of contributing)
2. ITHP NYCPPF contributions
3. Extra 50% NYCPPF contributions
4. NYC DCP 457(b) plan and/or NYC DCP Roth 457(b) plan contributions
5. NYC DCP 401(k) plan and/or NYC DCP Roth 401(k) plan contributions

Note: Members that are eligible to participate in the NYCDCP 401(a) plan may want to contribute at least 1% of earnings to the NYCDCP 457(b) plan or NYCDCP 401(k) plan.

The advantage of contributing as much as possible to the NYCPPF before the NYCDCP is to take full advantage of the fixed rate of return (currently 8.25%) on members' NYCPPF ASF account. A larger ASF account at retirement affords the retiring NYPD member with greater flexibility. The member could elect to leave the funds with the NYCPPF for an increased monthly benefit or could elect to rollover the funds to a new retirement plan.

Summary

This chapter reviewed the different retirement plans offered by the NYC Deferred Compensation Plan (NYCDCP). In general, the NYCDCP is a suitable retirement plan while working, but depending on the type of retirement plan an individual participates in, the NYCDCP may not be the most advantageous in retirement.

The contribution and distribution rules of the various retirement plans can be overwhelming and confusing. Prior to receiving a distribution from any of the NYCDCP retirement plans, an individual should review the tax implications and penalties, if applicable. Additionally, the participant should review if it would be advantageous to transfer the account to a different retirement plan in order to receive a more favorable distribution.

Readers of this book, who have not retired from the NYPD, should consider contributing to the NYC DCP Roth 457(b) plan instead of the NYC DCP 457(b) plan. As reviewed in this chapter, the NYC DCP Roth 457(b) plan is funded with after-tax money and can provide federal and state non-taxable distributions in retirement.

CHAPTER 5
Union Annuity Plan

There are five unions (PBA, DEA, SBA, LBA, & CEA) that represent and assist NYPD members. The PBA, DEA, & SBA each have their own Union Annuity Plan, while the LBA and CEA share the same plan. Years ago, it was nearly impossible for a participant to find out how the Union Annuity Plan was invested. Today, the Union Annuity Plans are more transparent, have a self-directed option, and account statements are mailed or emailed in a timely manner.

The Union Annuity Plans are funded by the City of New York. The amount NYC contributes is based on the union and its contract negotiations. Union members are currently not permitted to make ongoing contributions although rollovers into the plan may be permitted at retirement. Participant account balances are 100% vested, which means participants receive the value of the account if they quit, are fired, or vest from the NYPD.

Note: This chapter is an overview of the Union Annuity Plans. Retiring or retired members should check with their own union for more detailed information.

Union Annuity Plan at Retirement
At retirement, the Union Annuity Plan participant will generally have three choices available.

- Distribution (total or partial)
- Rollover to another retirement plan
- Leave funds with the Union Annuity Plan

Distributions (total or partial)
Distributions from the Union Annuity Plan are subject to federal tax and in some cases a 10% early distribution penalty. Distributions are generally not subject to NYS/NYC taxes, but may

or may not be subject to taxation by other states. The 10% early distribution penalty applies to the Union Annuity Plan participant who receives a distribution if less than 59 ½ years old. There is an exception to the 10% early distribution penalty if the Union Annuity Plan participant retired from the NYPD at age 50 or older (age 50 rule). The following is an example of a retired NYPD DEA member who has decided to receive a full distribution from the DEA Union Annuity Plan.

Assumptions
- 45-year-old recently retired NYPD DEA member
- Full distribution of $25,000 DEA Union Annuity Plan
- NYS/NYC resident

Income tax implications
- Federal tax owed on full distribution amount of $25,000
- 20% federal tax withholding. The retiree receives a check in the amount of $20,000.
- 10% early distribution penalty; the retiree is less than 59 ½ years old. The 10% penalty is assessed when the retiree completes his/her federal tax return.
- No NYS/NYC taxes

Rollover to Another Retirement Plan

The Union Annuity Plan can be rolled over to various types of retirement plans if the retiree wishes. Rolling over the Union Annuity Plan may not be the wisest choice due to the possible loss of the non-taxable NYS/NYC distribution feature. Although, converting the Union Annuity Plan to a Roth IRA may be an attractive alternative for some retirees. The features and advantages of the Roth IRA are reviewed in a subsequent chapter.

Rollover to NYCDCP Special 401(k)

Some retiring or retired NYPD members choose to rollover their Union Annuity Plan to the NYCDCP Special 401(k). In some cases, the NYCDCP Special 401(k) would then contain the final withdrawal, VSF DROP, and the Union Annuity Plan. The NYCDCP Special 401(k) has the "age 50 rule" for those that are eligible and favorable NYS/NYC taxes upon distribution.

To take advantage of the favorable NYS/NYC taxes, the retiree or tax preparer will need to do a specific calculation. The calculation is <u>not</u> done by the NYCDCP.

Leave Funds with the Union Annuity Plan

Generally, if the funds in the Union Annuity Plan are not currently needed, it may make sense to leave the funds in the plan.

Rolling Over Funds into the Union Annuity Plan at Retirement

Some of the Union Annuity Plans allow members to rollover certain funds into the plan at retirement. The funds that are commonly rolled over into the Union Annuity Plan are the final withdrawal and the VSF DROP. The primary reason why retiring NYPD members elect to do this is to retain the NYS/NYC non-taxable feature of the rolled over funds. Before performing the rollover, the retiring member should review the investment choices offered in their Union Annuity Plan in order to determine if the choices are appropriate for their situation. In addition, the fees and expenses of the Union Annuity Plan should be reviewed as well as the distribution choices.

Are the Union Annuity Plans Invested in Annuities?

The Union Annuity Plans are generally <u>not</u> invested in annuity products. Union Annuity Plan participants can select different types of mutual funds inside the plan based on the participant's risk tolerance. The Union Annuity Plans may offer a stable income fund, index funds, actively managed funds, balanced funds, etc. If the participant does not make changes to their investments, the contributions made by NYC are deposited into a "default fund".

Recently, the LBA/CEA Union Annuity Plan started to offer participants the ability to purchase immediate or deferred fixed annuities inside the plan. This type of investment may be suitable for the participant who desires a set dollar amount of income over a specified period. There are many advantages and disadvantages to a fixed annuity and the participant should fully understand the product before purchasing.

CHAPTER 6
IRA & Roth IRA

This chapter will provide a general overview of IRAs and Roth IRAs as they pertain to active and retired NYPD members. IRAs and Roth IRAs can be become complicated; therefore, this chapter is limited to tax and retirement planning topics that active or retired NYPD members may find useful. This chapter will not review advanced IRA issues, such as leaving IRA assets to a trust beneficiary or self-directed IRAs (investing in alternative assets).

IRAs

Individual Retirement Arrangements/Accounts (IRAs) were first created in 1974 when the Employee Retirement Income Security Act (ERISA) became law. During the early years, IRAs were restricted to those workers who were not already covered by a qualified employment-based retirement plan. In 1981, the Economic Recovery Tax Act became law which permitted all taxpayers less than 70½ years old to contribute to an IRA. Then, in 1986, the Tax Reform Act changed IRAs again. The IRA deduction was phased out for taxpayers (spouses) with higher incomes and covered by an employer retirement plan. The next significant change to the IRA was a result of the Economic Growth and Tax Relief Reconciliation Act of 2001 (EGTRA). EGTRA allowed an IRA annual contribution of $5,000 per taxpayer or $6,000 if age 50 or older. For calendar year 2019, taxpayers are permitted to contribute $6,000 ($7,000 if 50 or older) to an IRA. Whether the IRA contribution is deductible depends on the taxpayer's total income and whether the taxpayer or spouse is an active participant in an employer sponsored retirement plan. EGTRA also permits employers to establish "deemed IRAs" for its employees. Deemed IRAs are separate accounts within the governmental plan and are generally treated as if they are a "regular" IRAs or "regular" Roth IRAs. NYCDCP offers deemed IRAs & Roth IRAs for NYC employees and retirees.

IRA Contributions

Most active NYPD members do not contribute to an IRA due to the availability of various retirement plans (pension, 457(b), 401(k), etc.). Table #45 displays the 2019 phaseout ranges for a taxpayer to receive an IRA deduction.

TABLE #45

IRA Deductibility 2019 Phase-out Ranges

Filing Status	Phaseout Ranges
Single & has employer retirement plan	$64,000 to $74,000
Married & has employer retirement plan	$103,000 to $123,000
Married & spouse has employer retirement plan	$193,000 to $203,000
Married filing separate & has employer retirement plan	$0 to $10,000

The phaseout ranges limit the deductibility of the IRA contribution, but any taxpayer less than 70½ years old with earned income can contribute to an IRA. For example, if a 50-year-old NYPD employee has total income of $125,000, an IRA contribution is permitted, but there will be no deduction for the contribution. Many tax and financial professionals refer to this type of contribution as a "non-deductible" IRA contribution. When a taxpayer makes a non-deductible IRA contribution, they are using after-tax funds, the contribution is reported on IRS form 8606, and the taxpayer is responsible to keep track of the after-tax funds inside of the IRA. Even without receiving a deduction for the IRA contribution, the taxpayer may achieve tax-deferred growth or appreciation of the funds contributed.

Taxpayers can contribute to an IRA up until the due date of the federal tax return (generally, April 15, <u>not</u> including extensions). The following is an example of a married couple who have prepared their tax return and are trying to determine if a deductible IRA will provide tax savings.

Chapter 6: IRA & Roth IRA

- 52-year-old active NYPD employee
- 53-year-old spouse does not work
- Total income of $190,000

In this example, the NYPD employee will not receive a deduction for an IRA contribution, but the spouse is eligible for a $7,000 deductible IRA. Table #46 (based on tax year 2019) compares contributing to the spousal IRA vs. not contributing.

TABLE #46
IRA Contribution Tax Savings

Item	IRA Contribution	No IRA Contribution
Total Income	$190,000	$190,000
IRA Contribution	$7,000	$0
Adjusted Gross Income	$183,000	$190,000
Standard Deduction	$24,400	$24,400
Taxable Income	$158,600	$165,600
Tax	$26,609	$28,149
Tax Savings	$1,540	$0

IRA Distributions

Distributions from an IRA prior to age 59½ are subject to a 10% early distribution penalty, unless an exception applies. Distributions are taxed as ordinary income at the federal level and state level, if applicable. A taxpayer must begin to take distributions from an IRA by April 1 following the calendar year he or she reaches age 70½. It is important to note that, even if a taxpayer is still working at age 70½, the IRS requires distributions from an IRA.

IRA Exceptions to 10% Early Distribution Penalty

Taxpayers should be aware of the many exceptions to the 10% early distribution penalty for withdrawals from an IRA that occur prior to age 59½. The following are the more common exceptions to the 10% penalty.

- Distribution due to the total and permanent disability* of the IRA owner
- Distribution to pay for higher education expenses of IRA owner, spouse, child, or grandchild
- Distribution of up to $10,000 for a first-time home purchase
- After death of the IRA owner
- Series of substantial equal periodic payments
- Distribution due to an IRS levy

> **Author's Tip**
>
> IRS Form 5329 is used to report to the IRS an exception to the 10% early distribution penalty if not reported on IRS Form 1099-R. For example, a plan administrator may not know if a plan participant meets the IRS definition of disability and codes the IRS form 1099-R as code 1 in box #7 (penalty applies). In that case, if the taxpayer meets the IRS definition of disability, IRS form 5329 should be prepared to claim the exception.

Isolating IRA Tax-Free Basis Strategy

As explained earlier, if a taxpayer has made non-deductible IRA contributions to an IRA, some of the IRA contains after-tax money. As per IRS IRA rules, a taxpayer is not permitted to remove the non-taxable amount by itself, and any distribution taken is a pro-rata portion of the before-tax and after-tax money. There is a strategy that is available for NYCDCP members to remove just the non-taxable money and is best explained via an example.

Assume a 60-year-old NYPD retiree has an IRA balance of $100,000, which consists of $40,000 after-tax funds and $60,000 before-tax funds. If the retiree wanted to isolate the after-tax money, he could direct the IRA custodian to directly rollover the pre-tax portion ($60,000) of the IRA into the NYCDCP 401(k) plan. If the retiree does not have a NYCDCP 401(k), it can be established even though he or she is retired. After the rollover is completed, the IRA would only contain after-tax money and then the retiree could withdraw the after-tax money ($40,000) without a tax consequence.

---

* The IRS definition of disability is generally not the same definition used by the NYCPPF.

IRA 60-Day Rollover Rule

The IRA 60-day rollover rule seems simple enough, but it often causes problems for taxpayers. Additionally, in 2015, the IRS implemented new rules causing even more confusion and more ways for taxpayers to not be compliant. In general, the new rule states that a taxpayer is only permitted to perform one IRA 60-day rollover within a 365-day period. For example, assume a taxpayer who needs a short term "loan" removes $50,000 from his or her IRA. To avoid taxation on the $50,000, the taxpayer re-deposits the funds back into the IRA within 60 days. The taxpayer has satisfied the IRA 60-day rollover rule and is not permitted to do another 60-day rollover for 365 days.

The IRA 60-day rollover rule applies to IRA to IRA rollovers, but it does not apply to trustee-to-trustee transfers. Also, the one 60-day rollover rule in a 365-day period does not apply to rollovers from a retirement plan (457(b), 401(k), etc.) to an IRA.

Inherited IRA Distribution Rules

The distribution rules of Inherited IRAs often cause confusion among taxpayers. Upon the death of an IRA owner, distributions to a beneficiary are based on whether the beneficiary is a spouse or a non-spouse, the age of the deceased account holder, and may be limited by the distribution rules of the custodian (brokerage company, bank, etc.) of the IRA. Some taxpayers that received an IRA upon the death of the owner are often not aware that distributions may be required.

A spouse beneficiary may have the following four options available if the deceased IRA account holder was under 70½ years old.

1. Transfer the IRA to the spouse's own IRA, or the spouse creates a new IRA
2. Open an Inherited IRA and use life-expectancy method for distributions
3. Open an Inherited IRA and use five-year method for distributions
4. Receive lump-sum distribution

A spouse beneficiary may have the following three options available if the deceased IRA account holder was over 70½ years old.

1. Transfer the IRA to the spouse's own IRA, or the spouse creates a new IRA
2. Open an Inherited IRA and use life-expectancy method for distributions
3. Receive lump-sum distribution

A non-spouse beneficiary may have the following three options available if the deceased IRA account holder was under 70½ years old.

1. Open an Inherited IRA and use life-expectancy method for distributions
2. Open an Inherited IRA and use five-year method for distributions
3. Receive lump-sum distribution

A non-spouse beneficiary may have the following two options available if the deceased IRA account holder was over 70½ years old.

1. Open an Inherited IRA and use life-expectancy method for distributions
2. Receive lump-sum distribution

Roth IRAs

The 1997 Tax Relief Act created the Roth IRA, named after Senator William Roth. Since contributions to a Roth IRA are made with after-tax money, there is no deduction from income like the IRA.

The Roth IRA is the ultimate wealth-building retirement plan. Simply, the Roth IRA is funded with after-tax money, grows tax-deferred, and distributions are non-taxable after certain conditions are met. There are no required minimum distributions at age 70½ for the account owner while alive, which makes the Roth IRA an attractive and cost-effective estate planning mechanism. The conditions to receive non-taxable distributions are that the participant is age 59½ or older (or disabled/deceased) and the Roth IRA has been established for five years. If eligible and if they do not already have a Roth IRA, active & retired NYPD members should consider establishing and funding a Roth IRA to start the five-year time requirement. There are three methods available to fund a Roth IRA: annual contributions, rollovers, and conversions.

Roth IRA Annual Contributions

Making an annual contribution to a Roth IRA is permitted if the taxpayer has earnings that are either less than or within a specific range of the IRS phaseout range. The phaseout ranges for year 2019 are as follows.

> - Filing status of single = $122,000 to $137,000
> - Filing status of joint = $193,000 to $203,000
> - Filing status of married filing separately = $0 to $10,000

Currently, a taxpayer who is less than 50 years old can contribute $6,000 per year to a Roth IRA. A taxpayer that is 50 years old or older is eligible to contribute $7,000 per year to a Roth IRA. A Roth IRA contribution can be made during the period from January 1 of the current year up until the due date of the federal tax return (generally, April 15, <u>not</u> including extensions). Unlike the IRA, a Roth contribution can be made by a taxpayer 70½ or older if they have earned income. Contributions to a Roth IRA are not reported on the tax return and are not deductible.

It should be noted that for a taxpayer to contribute to a Roth IRA they must have earnings. In other words, if a NYPD retiree is only receiving pension income, an annual contribution to a Roth IRA would <u>not</u> be permitted.

"Back-Door" Roth IRA Contribution

The back-door Roth IRA contribution is a strategy used by taxpayers whose earnings are greater than the Roth IRA annual income contribution limits. This tax "loophole" is reviewed in the Advanced Tax and Retirement Planning chapter.

Rollovers to a Roth IRA

At retirement, NYPD members may have final withdrawal funds from the NYCPPF, VSF DROP funds, or other retirement plans available to be rolled over to a Roth IRA. By electing this type of rollover, the retiree would be subject to taxation in the current year. This option may be suitable for the retiree who would rather pay the taxes owed today than in the future. <u>Prior</u> to rolling over funds to a Roth IRA, it is very important that the pre-retiree calculate an estimate of the taxes owed at both the federal and state level, if applicable. Additionally, if the pre-retiree has multiple sources to choose from, it can become complicated choosing the most tax-efficient method.

Conversions

Conversion of a retirement plan to a Roth IRA is similar to a rollover to a Roth IRA, except for most, the conversion occurs at some point after separating from service (retirement). The basic premise of a conversion is that the retiree decides to convert pre-tax retirement plan assets (IRA, 457(b), 401(k), etc.) into a Roth IRA. In the past, conversions were only permitted if the taxpayer had income less than $100,000. The income tax laws changed in 2010, which allows anyone, regardless of income, to convert retirement plan assets to a Roth IRA. While an annual contribution to a Roth IRA requires earnings (compensation), conversions do not. How do these conversions work? The best way to explain a conversion is to go through a simple example.

Assumptions
- 50-year-old married NYPD retiree
- Pension = $80,000
- NYCDCP 401(k) plan balance = $75,000
- 50-year-old spouse W2 earnings = $35,000

If the retiree decides to convert the entire NYCDCP 401(k) plan balance ($75,000) at once into a Roth IRA, the couple's total income for the year would be $190,000. The $75,000 converted to a Roth IRA would be subject to ordinary income tax in the year of the conversion. Alternatively, the retiree could choose to convert only $10,000 of the $75,000 per year to possibly lessen the effect of income taxes. Ideally, funds (cash) should be available to pay the income taxes due so the entire amount converted can go into the Roth IRA. Prior to completing a conversion, the retiree should calculate an estimate of the taxes owed at both the federal and state level, if applicable. Additionally, if the pre-retiree has multiple retirement plans to choose from, it can become complicated choosing the most tax-efficient method. A IRA conversion may be either partially or fully taxable and is reported on IRS form 8606.

Recharacterizations of Conversions-No Longer Permitted

Prior to the 2017 Tax Cuts & Jobs Act (TCJA), taxpayers were permitted to recharacterize a Roth conversion. Basically, a recharacterization was a "do-over" and the taxpayer was able to treat the conversion as if it never happened. Taxpayers often performed a recharacterization when the Roth IRA dropped in value after the conversion. Since TCJA eliminated the ability for taxpayers to recharacterize a Roth conversion, retirees should carefully review the investments they are converting.

Roth IRA Distributions

The main feature of a Roth IRA is non-taxable distributions once two rules are satisfied: the taxpayer must be over 59½ years old, and the Roth IRA has been established for five taxable years. The first rule is easy to understand, while many taxpayers get confused regarding the five-year rule that applies to Roth IRAs. The five-year rule means that five tax years must pass from the first contribution to the Roth IRA to receive a distribution of the earnings without incurring taxes. Although generally five tax years must pass before earnings can be distributed tax-free, <u>contributions</u> to a Roth IRA can be removed tax-free and penalty-free at any time.

For example, assume a taxpayer contributes $5,500 to a Roth IRA on April 1, 2019 (for tax year 2018). The five-year rule would be satisfied as of, January 1, 2023. In this example, the initial contribution was only in the Roth IRA for three years and nine months, but it still satisfied the five-year rule due to tax years being used. At any time, the taxpayer could remove the $5,500 without incurring taxes or a penalty.

Roth IRA distributions can be become very confusing for taxpayers due to the specific ordering rules established by the IRS. In general, Roth IRA distributions are distributed in the following order.

1. Regular contributions
2. Conversion and rollover contributions
3. Earnings on contributions

As previously reviewed, regular contributions can be removed tax- and penalty-free at any time. For conversions and rollovers, distributions are taken on a first-in, first-out basis. The earnings on contributions are distributed only after all contributions, conversions, and rollovers have been distributed. To avoid taxation on the earnings, the Roth IRA distribution must be a qualified distribution. A qualified distribution occurs when the taxpayer has satisfied the five-year rule and the taxpayer is age 59½ or older or due to the Roth IRA owner's death or disability. The following are a few examples of Roth IRA distributions.

Example #1 is a 45-year-old taxpayer who has contributed $5,500 to a Roth in 2018. In 2019, the Roth IRA has appreciated to $7,000, and the taxpayer decides to take a total distribution of the Roth IRA. The taxpayer would not owe any taxes on the original $5,500 contribution, but the earnings ($1,500) would be subject to taxes and a 10% early distribution penalty.

Example #2 is a 45-year-old taxpayer who converted $25,000 of his NYCDCP 401(k) plan to a newly established Roth IRA in 2018. In 2019, the Roth IRA has appreciated to $30,000, and the taxpayer decides to take a total distribution of the Roth IRA. The taxpayer would not owe any taxes on the converted amount ($25,000), but the taxpayer would be subject to the 10% early distribution penalty on the $25,000. Additionally, the taxpayer would be subject to taxes and a 10% early distribution penalty on the earnings portion ($5,000).

Example #3 is a 60-year-old taxpayer who has a Roth IRA that has been funded with annual contributions of $13,000 and a conversion from the NYCDCP 401(k) plan in the amount of $40,000. To keep the example simple, the Roth IRA was established and funded for five taxable years and the conversion also satisfied the five-year rule. Since the taxpayer has satisfied the rules for a qualified distribution, all distributions are non-taxable and penalty-free.

Inherited Roth IRA Distributions

Upon the death of a Roth IRA owner, distributions to a beneficiary are based on whether the beneficiary is a spouse or a non-spouse and may be limited by the distribution rules of the custodian (brokerage company, bank, etc.) of the Roth IRA.

A spouse beneficiary may have the following four options available.

1. Transfer Roth IRA to the spouse's own Roth IRA, or the spouse creates a new Roth IRA
2. Open an inherited Roth IRA and use life-expectancy method for distributions
3. Open an inherited Roth IRA and use five-year method for distributions
4. Receive lump-sum distribution

A non-spouse beneficiary may have the following three options available.

1. Open an inherited Roth IRA and use life-expectancy method for distributions
2. Open an inherited Roth IRA and use five-year method for distributions
3. Receive lump-sum distribution

Wealth Building Power of the Roth IRA

Besides the non-taxable feature of distributions, many people are attracted to the Roth IRA due to its estate planning attributes. The Roth IRA is a straightforward and cost-effective strategy to leave money to the next generation. One of the significant advantages of a Roth IRA is that there are no required minimum distributions throughout the lifetime of the owner. In other words, the Roth IRA owner can decide to not take any money out of the Roth IRA and leave the entire account balance to a beneficiary(ies). The Roth IRA is the only retirement plan that has this feature; the 457(b), Roth 457(b), 401(k), Roth 401(k), and the regular IRA generally all require minimum distributions at age 70½. Using the assumptions, table #47 displays the benefits of the Roth IRA when the spouse is the beneficiary.

Assumptions
- 50-year-old Roth IRA owner
- Beginning balance of Roth IRA is $75,000
- Rate of return is 5%
- Roth IRA owner does not receive any distributions during lifetime
- 75-year-old Roth IRA owner dies
- Beneficiary: Spouse 75 years old at time Roth IRA owner's death. The Roth IRA is transferred and treated as "her own" Roth IRA.
- Spouse receives $20,000 distribution per year beginning at age 75
- Spouse is age 85 at death

TABLE #47

Roth IRA Wealth Building-Spouse Beneficiary

Age of Roth IRA Owner	Age of Spouse	Required Minimum Distribution	Distribution	Value of Roth IRA
50	50	N/A	N/A	$75,000
51	51	N/A	N/A	$78,750
52	52	N/A	N/A	$82,688
53	53	N/A	N/A	$86,822
54	54	N/A	N/A	$91,163
55	55	N/A	N/A	$95,722
56	56	N/A	N/A	$100,507
57	57	N/A	N/A	$105,533
58	58	N/A	N/A	$110,809
59	59	N/A	N/A	$116,350
60	60	N/A	N/A	$122,167
61	61	N/A	N/A	$128,275
62	62	N/A	N/A	$134,689
63	63	N/A	N/A	$141,424
64	64	N/A	N/A	$148,495
65	65	N/A	N/A	$155,920
66	66	N/A	N/A	$163,716
67	67	N/A	N/A	$171,901
68	68	N/A	N/A	$180,496
69	69	N/A	N/A	$189,521
70	70	$0	$0	$198,997
71	71	$0	$0	$208,947
72	72	$0	$0	$219,395
73	73	$0	$0	$230,364
74	74	$0	$0	$241,882
75	75	$0	$20,000	$233,977
N/A	76	$0	$20,000	$225,676
N/A	77	$0	$20,000	$216,960
N/A	78	$0	$20,000	$207,808

Chapter 6: IRA & Roth IRA

Age of Roth IRA Owner	Age of Spouse	Required Minimum Distribution	Distribution	Value of Roth IRA
N/A	79	$0	$20,000	$198,198
N/A	80	$0	$20,000	$188,108
N/A	81	$0	$20,000	$177,514
N/A	82	$0	$20,000	$166,389
N/A	83	$0	$20,000	$154,709
N/A	84	$0	$20,000	$142,444
N/A	85	$0	$20,000	$129,567

Reviewing table #47, the original Roth IRA owner started a $75,000 Roth IRA at age 50 and was able to grow the account to $241,882 by age 74. There were no required minimum distributions from age 70 ½ till death at age 75. The spouse received the Roth IRA at age 75 and decided to take a distribution of $20,000 per year. The spouse received $20,000 per year from age 75 till death at age 85. The $20,000 per year (total distribution of $220,000) was received tax-free. At the spouse's death, there was still $129,567 in the Roth IRA available for a beneficiary(ies).

Let's see what happens if we continue the example to include a 20-year-old beneficiary (grandchild). As per the rules of the Roth IRA, the beneficiary would be required to receive at least a minimum distribution from the Roth IRA. The required minimum distribution would also be non-taxable to the beneficiary.

Assumptions
- 20-year-old beneficiary
- Value of Roth IRA when received is $129,567
- Rate of return is 5%
- Required minimum distributions

TABLE #48

Roth IRA Wealth Building-Grandchild Beneficiary

Age of Roth IRA Beneficiary	Required Minimum Distribution	Value of Roth IRA
20	N/A	$129,567
21	$2,191	$133,854
22	$2,300	$138,247
23	$2,415	$142,744
24	$2,536	$147,345
25	$2,658	$152,054
26	$2,791	$156,865
27	$2,931	$161,778
28	$3,072	$166,795
29	$3,225	$171,909
30	$3,387	$177,118
31	$3,549	$182,425
32	$3,727	$187,820
33	$3,913	$193,298
34	$4,109	$198,854
35	$4,305	$204,492
36	$4,520	$210,196
37	$4,746	$215,959
38	$4,973	$221,785
39	$5,221	$227,653
40	$5,482	$233,553
41	$5,743	$239,487
42	$6,030	$245,431
43	$6,332	$251,371
44	$6,632	$257,308
45	$6,963	$263,210
46	$7,292	$269,079
47	$7,636	$274,897
48	$8,018	$280,624

Chapter 6: IRA & Roth IRA

Age of Roth IRA Beneficiary	Required Minimum Distribution	Value of Roth IRA
49	$8,395	$286,260
50	$8,789	$291,784
51	$9,200	$297,173
52	$9,660	$302,371
53	$10,111	$307,379
54	$10,582	$312,166
55	$11,073	$316,701
56	$11,587	$320,949
57	$12,079	$324,918
58	$12,636	$328,528
59	$13,217	$331,738
60	$13,822	$334,502
61	$14,395	$336,833
62	$15,050	$338,625
63	$15,663	$339,892
64	$16,371	$340,516
65	$17,026	$340,516
66	$17,700	$339,842
67	$18,394	$338,440
68	$19,106	$336,257
69	$19,835	$333,234
70	$20,582	$329,314
71	$21,213	$324,566
72	$21,987	$318,808
73	$22,618	$312,130
74	$23,244	$304,493
75	$23,860	$295,858

Reviewing table #48, the 20-year-old beneficiary received non-taxable distributions from age 21 through 75 years old. The total non-taxable distributions received by the beneficiary, over the 54-year period, were $544,891, with a remaining balance of $295,858 at the beneficiary's death. The beneficiary could have elected to receive the entire $129,567 tax-free at 20 years old, but that would have immediately ended the opportunity for ongoing distributions and appreciation of the Roth IRA.

This lengthy example demonstrated the wealth building and favorable tax treatment of the Roth IRA. The beginning balance of the original Roth IRA was only $75,000, while the total distributions were $764,891 ($220,000 to spouse and $544,891 to a grandchild).

Summary

This chapter provided a general overview of IRAs and Roth IRAs. Many active NYPD employees may not be contributing to an IRA or Roth IRA due to contributions to the NYCPPF and NYCDCP. For NYPD retirees, the IRA may be utilized for rollovers and in some cases to make annual contributions. Prior to taking a distribution from an IRA, the taxpayer less than 59½ years old should review the exceptions to the 10% early distribution penalty.

Under current law, the Roth IRA is often considered the ultimate retirement wealth builder and provides non-taxable distributions to both the owner and the beneficiary(ies.). The basic concept of the Roth IRA is quite simple: Contribute after-tax money, the account grows tax-deferred, and all the funds can be distributed tax-free after certain conditions are met.

CHAPTER 7
Social Security

The Social Security Act was signed into law on August 14th, 1935 during the Presidency of Franklin D. Roosevelt. For the next two years (1935-1937) employers and employees were registered in order to implement the program. In 1939, the Social Security Act was amended to include benefits to spouses and minor children of a retired worker and survivor benefits. In January 1940, the first monthly retirement check was issued to a retired legal secretary, Ida May Fuller. Over a 35-year retirement period, Ms. Fuller collected a total benefit of $22,000. Automatic Cost of Living Adjustments (COLA) was implemented in the year 1975. The largest COLA increase between the years 1975 and 2017 was the year 1980 with an increase of 14.3%.

This chapter will provide a general overview of the Social Security Retirement benefit; the Social Security Disability benefit is <u>not</u> reviewed. The actual calculation of the Social Security Retirement benefit will be reviewed but is somewhat complex. It is anybody's guess what the future of Social Security will be, and this chapter is based solely on current regulation.

Access Social Security Statement Online

Generally, the Social Security Administration no longer mails Social Security statements to most individuals. Although, individuals that are age 60 and older and are not receiving benefits will be mailed a Social Security statement. An individual's Social Security statement can be viewed online once an account has been verified and established. Establishing an account and reviewing the statement annually will enable an individual to inform the Social Security Administration of any omissions and/or mistakes. It should be noted that the estimated monthly retirement benefits listed on the statement may not be entirely accurate for a retired NYPD member who only earns part-time income or no longer is employed. When preparing the estimate, the Social

Security Administration assumes using average earnings over an individual's working lifetime and that the individual will continue to work and earn the prior year's wages.

Social Security Statement Retirement Benefit Basics

When an individual starts to plan for Social Security Retirement benefits, there are a few important terms that must be understood.

- Full Retirement Age (FRA)
    - also referred to as Normal Retirement Age
    - individual receives the full retirement benefit from Social Security
    - FRA varies by what year an individual was born
        - Year of birth 1960 or later, FRA at 67 years old
        - Year of birth 1959, FRA at 66 years/10 months old
        - Year of birth 1958, FRA at 66 years/8 months old
        - Year of birth 1957, FRA at 66 years/6 months old
        - Year of birth 1956, FRA at 66 years/4 months old
        - Year of birth 1955, FRA at 66 years/2 months old
        - Year of birth 1943-54, FRA at 66 years old
- Primary Insurance Amount (PIA)
    - PIA is received by individuals who start benefits at FRA
- Delayed retirement credits
    - individuals receive a larger retirement benefit if they delay payments until after FRA
- Reduced retirement benefits
    - individual receives retirement benefits before FRA

Calculation of the Social Security Retirement Benefit

The actual calculation of the Social Security Retirement benefit is somewhat complicated. The calculation requires a maximum earnings limit, actual earnings, index factors, indexed earnings, and "bend points". The following is an example of an estimated Social Security Retirement benefit for a person born in 1956 (62 years old in 2018), started working at age 18 (year 1974), and retired at age 56 (year 2012). Table #49 displays the person's earnings history over their working career.

TABLE #49
Social Security Retirement Benefit Example

Year	Maximum Earnings	Actual Earnings	Index Factor	Indexed Earnings
1974	$13,200	$4,000	6.06	$24,240
1975	$14,100	$4,500	5.64	$25,380
1976	$15,300	$15,000	5.27	$79,050
1977	$16,500	$16,000	4.98	**$79,680**
1978	$17,700	$18,000	4.61	**$82,980**
1979	$22,900	$21,000	4.24	**$89,040**
1980	$25,900	$24,000	3.89	**$93,360**
1981	$29,700	$25,000	3.53	**$88,250**
1982	$32,400	$28,000	3.35	**$93,800**
1983	$35,700	$33,000	3.19	**$105,270**
1984	$37,800	$37,800	3.02	**$114,156**
1985	$39,600	$39,600	2.89	**$114,444**
1986	$42,000	$42,000	2.81	**$118,020**
1987	$43,800	$43,800	2.64	**$115,632**
1988	$45,000	$45,000	2.52	**$113,400**
1989	$48,000	$48,000	2.42	**$116,160**
1990	$51,300	$50,000	2.31	**$115,500**
1991	$53,400	$51,000	2.23	**$113,730**
1992	$55,500	$55,000	2.12	**$116,600**
1993	$57,600	$56,000	2.10	**$117,600**
1994	$60,600	$60,000	2.05	**$123,000**
1995	$61,200	$61,200	1.97	**$120,564**
1996	$62,700	$62,700	1.88	**$117,876**
1997	$65,400	$65,400	1.77	**$115,758**
1998	$68,400	$68,400	1.69	**$115,596**
1999	$72,600	$72,600	1.60	**$116,160**
2000	$76,200	$76,200	1.51	**$115,062**
2001	$80,400	$80,400	1.48	**$118,992**
2002	$84,900	$84,900	1.46	**$123,954**

Year	Maximum Earnings	Actual Earnings	Index Factor	Indexed Earnings
2003	$87,000	$87,000	1.43	**$124,410**
2004	$87,900	$87,900	1.37	**$120,423**
2005	$90,000	$90,000	1.32	**$118,800**
2006	$94,200	$94,200	1.26	**$118,692**
2007	$97,500	$97,500	1.20	**$117,000**
2008	$102,000	$102,000	1.18	**$120,360**
2009	$106,800	$106,800	1.20	**$128,160**
2010	$106,800	$106,800	1.17	**$124,956**
2011	$106,800	$106,800	1.13	**$120,684**
2012	$110,100	$0	1.10	$0
2013	$113,700	$0	1.08	$0
2014	$117,000	$0	1.05	$0
2015	$118,500	$0	1.01	$0
2016	$118,500	$0	1.00	$0
2017	$127,200	$0	1.00	$0

Steps to Estimate the Social Security Retirement Benefit

Step #1: Enter actual earnings, but not more than maximum earnings.

Step #2: Multiply actual earnings by index factor to get indexed earnings.

Step #3: From the indexed earnings column choose the 35 years with the highest amounts (indicated in bold).

Step #4: Add the 35 years of indexed earnings.
= $3,948,069

Step #5: Divide $3,948,069 by 420 = $9,400

Step #6: Multiply the first $895 of $9,400 by 90% = $805

Step #7: Multiply $9,400 over $895, and less than $5,397 by 32% = $1,441

Step #8: $9,400 - $5,397 x 15% = $600

Step #9: Add $805 + $1,441 + 600 = $2,846. This is the estimated benefit at full retirement age (66 years and 4 months).

Step #10: Multiply $2,846 by 73.33% = $2,087. This is the estimated benefit at age 62.

Chapter 7: Social Security

<u>Note</u>: Steps 6, 7, and 8 are known as "bend points" and generally change every year.

Fortunately, the Social Security Administration website has various calculators available to help with calculating the Social Security Retirement benefit.

Receiving the Social Security Retirement Benefit Early

Most individuals elect to receive Social Security Retirement benefits before full retirement age. Many begin at the earliest opportunity (62 years old) because they need the money to live on, do not fully understand the benefits of delaying, or have convinced themselves that the Social Security system is going to collapse.

Depending on what year an individual was born, the reduction to the Social Security Retirement benefit may be 70-75% of the PIA when benefits are received at 62 years old. The following is an example of an individual with a full retirement age (FRA) of 66 and four months and a PIA of $2,500.

TABLE #50

Reduced Social Security Retirement Benefit Example (PIA = $2,500)

Age	Percentage	Benefit
62	73.3%	$1,832
62 + 1 month	73.8%	$1,845
62 + 4 months	75%	$1,875
63	78.3%	$1,957
63 + 6 months	81.1%	$2,028
64	84.4%	$2,110
64 + 6 months	87.8%	$2,195
65	91.1%	$2,277
65 + 6 months	94.4%	$2,360
66	97.8%	$2,445
66 + 4 months	100%	$2,500

Even though individuals who elect reduced retirement benefits receive COLA, these adjustments have not been very significant recently.

Delaying the Social Security Retirement Benefit

For many retired NYPD members, it may make sense to receive distributions from a retirement plan and delay receiving Social Security Retirement benefits beyond FRA. For every month the Social Security Retirement benefit is delayed, the retiree receives a percentage increase until age 70. The following is an example of an individual with a full retirement age (FRA) of 66 and a PIA of $1,800.

- Benefits commence at 66 years old = $1,800
    - no benefit increase
- Benefits commence at 66 years and 3 months old = $1,836
    - increase of 2%
- Benefits commence at 67 years old = $1,944
    - increase of 8%
- Benefits commence at 67 years and 6 months old = $2,016
    - increase of 12%
- Benefits commence at 68 years old = $2,088
    - increase of 16%
- Benefits commence at 68 years and 6 months old = $2,160
    - increase of 20%
- Benefits commence at 69 years old = $2,232
    - increase of 24%
- Benefits commence at 69 years and 6 months old = $2,304
    - increase of 28%
- Benefits commence at 70 years old = $2,376
    - increase of 32%

For every year the retirement benefit was delayed, the individual received an 8% increase to the PIA. Delaying the retirement benefit until 70 years old resulted in a 32% higher monthly benefit.

Summary Table: Reductions & Increases to PIA

TABLE #51	
Reductions & Increases to PIA	
Age When Retirement Benefits Are Claimed	*Amount of Retirement Benefit*
5 years before FRA	70% of PIA
4 years before FRA	75% of PIA
3 years before FRA	80% of PIA
2 years before FRA	86.67% of PIA
1 year before FRA	93.33% of PIA
At FRA	100% of PIA
1 year after FRA	108% of PIA
2 years after FRA	116% of PIA
3 years after FRA	124% of PIA
4 years after FRA	132% of PIA

Life Expectancy

Obviously, if an individual knew when they were going to die, they would know when to start receiving Social Security Retirement benefits. Since the death date is unknown, it may be beneficial for an individual (single person) to plan to live beyond 80 years old and delay the Social Security retirement benefit until 70 years old. Delaying the retirement benefit minimizes longevity risk. Simply put, the individual is trying to minimize the effects of living longer than expected.

Social Security Claiming Strategies

In 2015, President Obama signed the Bipartisan Budget Act of 2015 which eliminated two favorable Social Security claiming strategies. In general, the "File & Suspend" and "Restricted Application" strategies are no longer available.

Single Person

Generally, the Social Security claiming strategies for a single individual are straightforward and for the most part are based on the life expectancy of the individual. For example, if an individual (single person) expects to only live to 80 years old, claiming retirement benefits at age 62 would be optimal. Alternatively, if an individual expects to live well beyond 80 years old, claiming retirement benefits at age 70 would be ideal.

Married Couple

The Social Security claiming strategies for a married couple can be more complicated and varied. Married couples should consider the life expectancies of both spouse's when making the decision to receive or delay retirement benefits. Recently, there have been a few websites created that review various Social Security claiming strategies. Many of the websites require the user to enter personal information and pay a small fee to view the recommended strategies.

Unmarried Minor Children, Divorced, and Widow(er)

When an individual is insured by Social Security there are many instances where another individual may be able to claim a benefit. Believe it or not, it is even possible for a dependent grandchild to receive a benefit based on a grandparent's earnings record.

For children to receive a benefit, the parent would need to be qualified for Social Security Retirement benefits. The child (biological, adopted, or stepchild) would have to be unmarried and generally be less than 18 years old (a disabled child has different rules). The following is an example of a child receiving a benefit based on her parent's earnings record.

Assumptions
- Mary's age is 62, is a single parent, and has a PIA of $1,500 and her FRA is 66 years old
- Mary's adopted daughter, Jane, is 14 years old

Strategy
- Mary elects to receive a reduced benefit of $1,125 at 62 years old
- Jane receives $750 (half of Mary's PIA)
- Mary and Jane would receive a combined total of $1,875 per month until Jane becomes 18 years old. After Jane reaches 18 years old, Mary would continue to receive her $1,125.

The Social Security Retirement benefit rules regarding divorced individuals can be complicated. The following are a few highlights for a divorced individual utilizing the ex-spouse's earnings record.

- When benefits can commence is based on if the ex-spouse is living or deceased
- In most cases, marriage lasted 10 years or longer
- In most cases, individual did not re-marry; it doesn't matter if ex-spouse re-marries
- Individual is 62 years old or older
- Ex-spouse is entitled to Social Security Retirement benefits

In general, divorced spouse benefits are calculated the same way as regular spousal benefits. Divorced individuals should meet with Social Security personnel or a financial advisor that specializes in Social Security in order to determine retirement benefits that may apply for their situation.

A widow or widower may be able to claim Social Security Retirement benefits based on a deceased spouse's earnings record. The following are a few highlights for a widow(er) individual utilizing the deceased spouse's earnings record.

- Marriage lasted for at least nine months
- Did not remarry, unless the widow(er) remarried after age 60
- Spouse was Social Security "fully insured" at time of death
- Widow(er) must be at least 60 years old (or disabled and at least age 50)

Do-Over Options
The Social Security Administration offers two do-over options if a person changes their mind regarding when the retirement benefits were claimed.

Withdrawing Your Application
A person receiving Social Security Retirement benefits has up to 12 months to change their mind. For example, assume an individual decided to claim a reduced retirement benefit at age 62, but 11 months later regretted the decision. The individual could fill out Form SSA-521 to stop the retirement benefits. The following are a few highlights of this option.

- An application to withdraw can only be done once in a lifetime
- You must pay back (without interest) the benefits received
- Tax ramifications due to the repayment of benefits

Suspend Retirement Benefits

If a person has been receiving Social Security Retirement benefits for 12 months or more, the benefit can be suspended at FRA. After suspending the benefits, the person can choose when to restart the benefit up until age 70. For example, assume an individual (with an FRA of 66) decided to receive Social security Retirement benefits at age 62. The benefit is equal to $1,875 per month (75% of PIA). Once the individual reaches age 66, they can suspend the benefits. Suspending the benefits results in the individual receiving delayed retirement credits until age 70.

Summary

The purpose of this chapter was to provide the reader with a basic understanding of the Social Security Retirement benefit and the various terms. There are many variables that should be reviewed before an individual decides whether to begin Social Security Retirement benefits. For some it may make financial sense to receive benefits at 62 years old while for others delaying the benefit may be advantageous.

This chapter also provided information regarding the two do-over options that are available; withdrawing your application and suspending benefits.

CHAPTER 8
Taxes, Distribution Planning, & RMDs

When a NYPD employee gets ready to retire, an understanding of the various tax laws is critical. A mistake can be very costly and difficult if not impossible to correct. This chapter will review some of the common tax issues that retired NYPD members often encounter. Before some of the tax issues are reviewed, a brief overview is provided of the different types of tax preparers and the importance of selecting the right one.

Tax Preparers

This is one area where many NYPD members (retired and active) give themselves a lot of avoidable stress. Rule #1 is to locate a reputable, professional, and knowledgeable tax preparer. If you are still going to that tax preparer that works out of their basement and prepares tax returns with a pencil, time to move on. Yes, you will have to pay more, but it will be worth it in the long run. Of course, a good tax preparer needs to know general tax law, but the tax preparer should also be knowledgeable about the NYCPPF, NYC Deferred Compensation Plans, Union Annuity Plans, etc.

Tax Preparer Licenses/Certifications

Over the past couple of years, there has been a significant increase of IRS oversight in the tax preparation industry. The IRS has implemented various requirements to protect the tax paying public from unqualified and unethical tax preparers. Tax preparers are required to register with the IRS and obtain a Tax Preparer Identification Number (PTIN). In general, there are four types of tax preparers.

- Unenrolled tax preparer
- Enrolled Agent (EA)

- Certified Public Accountant (CPA)
- Attorney

Unenrolled Tax Preparer
The unenrolled tax preparer is any individual who is not an Enrolled Agent, CPA, or attorney. Unenrolled tax preparers often work for a store front tax preparation company (H&R Block, Liberty Tax, etc.) and <u>may</u> have limited experience and knowledge.

Enrolled Agent (EA)
An Enrolled Agent is a tax practitioner license granted by the U.S. Department of Treasury. The IRS refers to the enrolled agent as an elite status and is the highest credential the IRS awards. EAs' specialize in areas of taxation and are authorized to represent taxpayers before all administrative levels of the Internal Revenue Service in reference to audits, appeals, and collections. Enrolled agents, like attorneys and CPAs, have unlimited practice rights. This means they are unrestricted as to which taxpayers they can represent, what types of tax matters they can handle, and which IRS offices they can represent clients before. The following are the requirements to become and maintain enrolled agent status.

- Obtain a PTIN
- Pass a three-part comprehensive IRS test covering individual and business tax returns
- Pass a tax-compliance and suitability check
- Complete 72 hours of continuing education credits every three years

Certified Public Accountant (CPA)
The Certified Public Accountant is a designation granted by the American Institute of Certified Public Accountants. A CPA received their license from a state and has completed various education and experience requirements. A CPA may work in many areas of business and may not specialize in taxation.

Pension Federal Tax Withholding (W4P)

In most cases, federal income taxes are withheld from NYCPPF pension payments. This is one area where many NYPD members have difficulty understanding and correctly implementing. A question that is often asked is; what tax rate will I pay on my pension? This is not an easy question to answer since everyone's tax situation is different. For example, a single NYPD retired member who retires with a $50,000 pension and has no other earnings would be in a lower tax bracket than a married NYPD retired member who retires with a $50,000 pension and a spouse that earns $100,000. When a NYPD member goes to the NYCPPF for their retirement counseling session they will need to decide how much federal tax withholding will be deducted from their monthly pension check. This is an important decision because the retiree does not want to be in a position at tax time that not enough taxes were withheld. Retiring members may want to err on the side of caution and elect withholding that may be more than what they were withholding while working. If not enough or too much was withheld, the retiree can easily correct the withholding by mailing a new IRS form W4P to the NYCPPF.

Note: NYCPPF pensions are not subject to Social Security, Medicare, NYS, or NYC taxes.

State Taxation of NYCPPF Pensions

The NYPD retiree should carefully review the state and local taxes of an area they are considering retiring to. There are a handful of states that do not have a state individual income tax., but most states tax all or a portion of the pension. In most cases, the non-taxable portion of the accidental disability pension is not taxed by states, but there are exceptions (New Jersey). The payment of state and local income taxes on retirement income should not be taken lightly. As the NYPD retiree ages, taxes paid become a significant disadvantage as the pension decreases in value due to inflation. The following is a summary of how NYCPPF pensions are taxed at the state level.

Note: States often change personal income tax rules regarding pensions, and it is strongly suggested pre-retirees and retirees perform their own research prior to relocating.

States that do not have a personal income tax
- Alaska
- Florida
- Nevada
- South Dakota
- Texas
- Washington
- Wyoming

States that only tax interest and dividends
- New Hampshire
- Tennessee

States with a wide-ranging personal income tax

- Alabama
  - Full exclusion
- Arizona
  - No exclusion
- Arkansas
  - Exclusion of $6,000 per taxpayer
- California
  - No exclusion
- Colorado
  - 65 or older receive a $24,000 exclusion
  - 55 to 65 years old receive a $20,000
  - Spouses must qualify individually
- Connecticut
  - No exclusion
- Delaware
  - 60 or older receive a $12,500 exclusion
  - Less than 60 receive a $2,000 exclusion
  - Exclusions are for each taxpayer
- District of Columbia
  - No exclusion
- Georgia
  - 62 to 64 years of age may receive an exclusion of $35,000 per taxpayer ($70,000 joint).
  - 65 or older may receive an exclusion of $65,000
- Hawaii
  - Full exclusion
- Idaho
  - No exclusion
- Illinois
  - Full exclusion
- Indiana
  - No exclusion
- Iowa
  - 55 or older may receive an exclusion of $6,000 individual or $12,000 joint
- Kansas
  - No exclusion
- Kentucky
  - No exclusion
- Louisiana
  - Non-Louisiana pension exclusion of $6,000 (single) or $12,000 (joint) if 65 years or older
- Maine
  - Generally, no exclusion
- Maryland
  - 65 or older (or totally disabled) exemption up to $29,000
- Massachusetts
  - if over 59 ½ years old, exclude up to $20,000
- Michigan
  - Has different rules based on the retiree's year of birth
  - Michigan Department of the Treasury issues a yearly chart explaining the individual income tax treatment for retirement benefits

- Minnesota
  - No exclusion, although age 65 or older may qualify for an exception up to $9,000 (single) or $18,000 (married-joint) if within income limits
- Mississippi
  - Full exclusion
- Missouri
  - A full exclusion may be available, but it is based on income limits, filing status, and may be reduced based on taxable Social Security benefits
- Montana
  - Minimal exclusion is reduced/eliminated based on federal adjusted gross income
- Nebraska
  - No exclusion
- New Jersey
  - 62 and older receive a $45,000 (single), $60,000 (joint), or $30,000 (separate) exclusion for tax year 2018
  - 62 and older receive a $60,000 (single), $80,000 (joint), or $40,000 (separate) exclusion for tax year 2019
  - 62 and older receive a $75,000 (single), $100,000 (joint), or $50,000 (separate) exclusion for tax year 2020
  - Exclusion subject to an income ceiling of $100,000
- New Mexico
  - No exclusion, but New Mexico does have an income exemption
  - 65 or older have an income exemption maximum of $8,000 (single) or $16,000 (joint) although phased out as income grows
  - Individual aged 100 or older fully exempt from New Mexico taxation unless claimed as a dependent
- New York
  - Full exclusion
- North Carolina
  - No exclusion
- North Dakota
  - No exclusion
- Ohio
  - No exclusion, although taxpayers may be eligible for a minimal tax credit
- Oklahoma
  - Exclusion of up to $10,000 per individual
  - A spouse must qualify individually
- Oregon
  - No exclusion, although those 62 or older may receive a credit based on income limits
- Pennsylvania
  - Full exclusion
- Rhode Island
  - No exclusion

- South Carolina
  - Less than 65 up to a $3,000 exclusion
  - Over 65 up to a $10,000 exclusion
- Utah
  - No exclusion, although a taxpayer 65 or older may receive a tax credit based on income limits
- Vermont
  - No exclusion
- Virginia
  - 75 or older up to $12,000 ($24,000 married joint)
  - From 65 to 74 years old, $12,000 deduction is reduced and phased out at higher income levels
- West Virginia
  - May be eligible to exclude up to $8,000 based on age
- Wisconsin
  - May be eligible to exclude up to $5,000 based on income limits

NYS Tax Advantages for NYPD Retirees

Retiring from the NYPD and remaining a NYS resident has some tax advantages. Currently, NYS has very favorable tax laws that benefit a retired NYPD member. The following retirement income is not taxed by NYS/NYC.

- Pension from the NYCPPF
- VSF payment from the NYCPPF
- Annuity distributions from SOC, SBA, DEA, & PBA
- Social Security Retirement & Disability benefits
- $20,000 Pension & Annuity Exclusion if over 59 ½ years old

NYS Pension & Annuity Exclusion

The NYS Pension & Annuity Exclusion is often misunderstood and incorrectly used by NYPD retirees. The NYS Pension & Annuity Exclusion is a NYS tax law that allows certain individuals to exclude a maximum of $20,000 per year from their NYS gross income due to a distribution from a retirement plan (457b, 401k, IRA, etc.). The following are the general rules an individual must meet in order to take advantage of this tax provision.

- Individual is over 59 ½ years old
  - in some cases, a beneficiary, of any age, may be able to take advantage of the exclusion
- Periodic distribution (not always)
- Distribution must be included in federal gross income

Note: Distributions from many (not all) retirement plans prior to 59 ½ years old are subject to NYS/NYC taxes.

Table #52 is an example of a 60-year-old NYS resident utilizing the $20,000 NYS Pension & Annuity Exclusion.

TABLE #52
NYS Pension & Annuity Exclusion

Item	Federal	NYS
Pension	$50,000	$50,000
NYCDCP 457(b) Periodic Distribution	$30,000	$30,000
Federal Adjusted Gross Income	$80,000	$80,000
NYS Pension Full Exclusion	N/A	-$50,000
NYS Pension & Annuity Exclusion	N/A	-$20,000
NYS Adjusted Gross Income	N/A	$10,000

$3,000 Health Insurance Premium Deduction

Eligible NYPD retirees are permitted to exclude up to $3,000 to pay for qualified health insurance premiums. To claim the exclusion, the health insurance premiums are deducted from amounts distributed from an eligible governmental plan and paid directly to the insurer. The health insurance premiums can be based on accident and health insurance or long-term insurance for the retired NYPD member and his or her spouse or dependents.

The IRS 1099-R form issued by the NYCPPF does not exclude the health insurance premiums paid, if any. In other words, box #2a of the IRS 1099-R form does not include the exclusion. It is the responsibility of the eligible taxpayer to report the reduction of gross income on the federal tax return. If the taxpayer qualifies for this exclusion, he or she should reduce the otherwise taxable amount of the pension by the amount excluded.

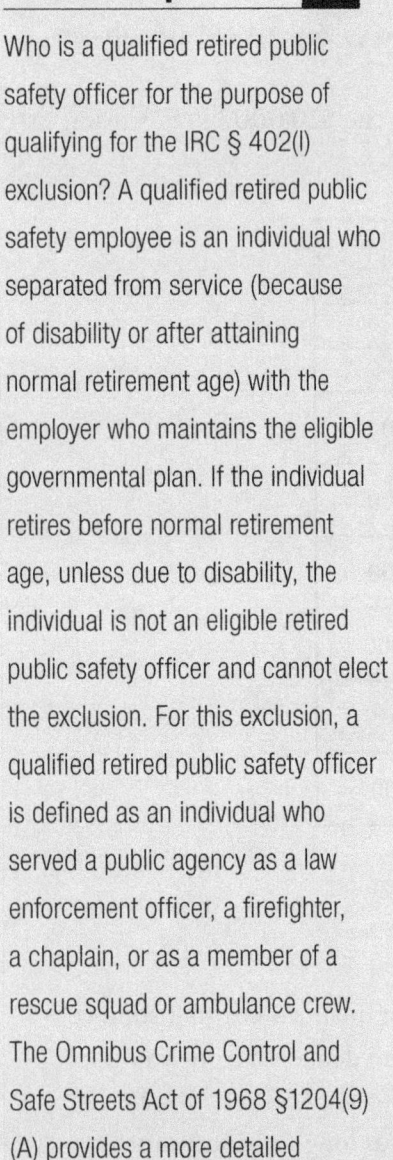

Is it possible to amend a federal tax return if the retired NYPD member did not claim the exclusion? Yes. Prior to amending the tax return, the taxpayer should carefully review the tax return to determine if amending may cause issues with the IRS. If a taxpayer finds mistakes with the original tax return, those mistakes should be fixed with the filing of the amended return. In general, taxpayers are permitted to amend a tax return within three years from the date the original return was filed (returns filed before the due date are considered filed on the due date) or within two years from the date you paid the tax, whichever is later. Currently, federal amended tax returns must be filed by paper, and each year a taxpayer is amending requires its own IRS form 1040X.

Depending on the amount of the health insurance premium that was not deducted and the taxpayer's overall tax situation, amending may be worthwhile. For example, a retired NYPD member's accountant was not familiar with the public safety officer's health insurance deduction and did not deduct the $3,000 premiums even though the taxpayer was eligible. After the taxpayer learned about this unique deduction, he hired a new accountant. The new accountant interviewed the taxpayer and determined that he was in fact eligible for the deduction. The new accountant also suggested that the taxpayer amend three years of tax returns to correctly claim the deduction he was entitled to. After the three amended returns were processed by the IRS, the taxpayer received a total refund of $2,747 plus interest.

> **Author's Tip**
>
> Who is a qualified retired public safety officer for the purpose of qualifying for the IRC § 402(l) exclusion? A qualified retired public safety employee is an individual who separated from service (because of disability or after attaining normal retirement age) with the employer who maintains the eligible governmental plan. If the individual retires before normal retirement age, unless due to disability, the individual is not an eligible retired public safety officer and cannot elect the exclusion. For this exclusion, a qualified retired public safety officer is defined as an individual who served a public agency as a law enforcement officer, a firefighter, a chaplain, or as a member of a rescue squad or ambulance crew. The Omnibus Crime Control and Safe Streets Act of 1968 §1204(9)(A) provides a more detailed definition of public safety officer.

Taxes & Retirement

It is often reported in newspapers and financial magazines that retirees in general are more than likely to be in a lower income tax bracket during retirement. This may not be true for some NYPD retirees. This may happen to some NYPD retirees due to a combination of the pension benefit, Social Security Retirement benefits, and distributions from retirement accounts. For these types of retirees, it very often becomes apparent when required minimum distributions (RMDs) take effect. Another item that is often overlooked is that retirees do not normally have many deductions (mortgage interest, property taxes, dependent children, etc.) which may result in paying more income taxes in retirement.

In the Case Studies chapter, Case Study #2 reviews a NYPD retiree who deferred significant amounts of money into the NYCDCP while working and will be subject to large RMDs.

NYC DCP 457(b) Tax Issues

As reviewed earlier, the 10% early distribution penalty does not apply to NYCDCP 457(b) distributions regardless of the retiree's age. The following are two examples of the tax implications of a distribution from the NYCDCP 457(b) plan.

Example 1:

Assumptions
- 48-year-old retired NYPD member
- Receives a one-time distribution of $30,000 from the NYC DCP 457(b) plan

Income tax implications
- No 10% early distribution penalty even though the retiree is less than 59 ½ years old
- Retiree will receive $24,000 from the NYCDCP. The NYCDCP is required by law to withhold 20% for federal tax from this type of distribution
- Retiree is subject to federal tax on the entire $30,000 distribution
- The $30,000 distribution is taxable by NYS and NYC, if applicable. In general, there is no NYS $20,000 pension/annuity exclusion for retirees less than 59 ½ years old.

Example 2:
Assumptions
- 62-year-old retired NYPD member
- Receives a periodic distribution of $30,000 from the NYCDCP 457(b) plan
- Does not receive any other distribution(s) from his retirement plans

Income tax implications
- Retiree will receive $24,000 from the NYCDCP. The NYCDCP is required by law to withhold 20% for federal tax from this type of distribution
- Retiree is subject to federal tax on the entire $30,000 distribution
- $10,000 of the $30,000 distribution is taxable by NYS and NYC, if applicable. The retiree was able to take advantage of the NYS $20,000 pension/annuity exclusion due to the fact he was over 59 ½ years old and the distribution was periodic.

Occasionally, retired NYPD members decide to withdraw a significant amount of money from their NYCDCP 457(b) plan for the purpose of buying a second home, paying off a mortgage, starting a business, etc. The retiree should calculate an estimate of what the tax implications (federal, state, and local) will be <u>before</u> requesting a distribution. Retirees that receive a large NYCDCP 457(b) distribution without calculating an estimate are unpleasantly surprised at tax time. The following is an example of a retiree who received a significant distribution from the NYCDCP 457(b) plan.

Assumptions
- 48-year-old retired NYPD member residing in NYS/NYC
- Receives a one-time distribution of $300,000 from the NYCDCP 457(b) plan
- Does not receive any other distribution(s) from his retirement plans

Income tax implications
- Retiree will receive $240,000 from the NYCDCP. The NYCDCP is required by law to withhold 20% for federal tax from this type of distribution.
- Retiree is subject to federal tax on the entire $300,000 distribution
- The entire $300,000 distribution is taxable by NYS and NYC. In general, there is no NYS $20,000 pension/annuity exclusion for retirees less than 59 ½ years old.

In this example, depending on the retiree's overall tax situation, the 20% federal tax withholding ($60,000) may not have been enough and the retiree will more than likely owe even more taxes at tax time. Additionally, the NYCDCP does not automatically withhold NYS/NYC taxes on distributions, therefore the retiree will more than likely owe significant NYS and NYC taxes at tax time.

Exceptions to 10% Early Distribution Penalty

NYPD retirees need to avoid this IRS imposed penalty whenever possible. Generally, the penalty is assessed when an individual receives a distribution from a retirement plan (does not apply to NYCDCP 457(b) distributions) and is less than 59 ½ years old. The penalty is an additional tax on the taxable amount of the money distributed. The penalty is added to the regular income taxes paid on the distribution when an individual's taxes are prepared. The following are some of the more common exceptions to the 10% early distribution penalty.

- Series of substantial equal periodic payments (72t)
- Distributions made to a beneficiary upon death of retirement plan owner
- Distributions due to retirement plan owner being totally and permanently disabled. Caution: the IRS does not use the same definition of disabled as the NYCPPF.
- Distributions from the NYCPPF and VSF DROP if retiree separated from service after 50 years old. The 50-year-old exception does not apply if the retiree rolls over the final withdrawal and the VSF DROP into an IRA and takes a distribution from the rollover IRA.
- Distributions from Union Annuity Plan if retiree separated from NYPD service after 50 years old
- Distributions from an <u>IRA</u> due to paying for college expenses for yourself, your spouse, your children, or grandchildren

NYCDCP & The Age 50 Rule

The NYCDCP has acknowledged that the "age 50 rule" applies to distributions from the 401(k) & 401(a) plans for retired NYPD members, but leaves it to the participant/taxpayer to correctly report it to the IRS. In the author's opinion, the NYCDCP has taken the easy way out instead of correctly reporting the distribution to the IRS on behalf of the participant. Due to the lack of help from the NYCDCP, some participants may incur the 10% early distribution penalty even though they qualify for the exception. Additionally, many accountants may not be familiar with this exception which may also cause the taxpayer to incur the penalty.

When a NYCDCP participant takes a distribution from their retirement plan(s), a 1099-R (IRS form) is generated in January of the following year. The form is issued to the participant and sent to the IRS/State. A significant problem with the 1099-R forms issued by the NYCDCP is that there is no indication on the form from which retirement plan (457(b), 401(k), etc.) the funds were distributed. A correctly prepared 1099-R form has a distribution code entered in Box #7. A code of "1" indicates an early distribution, no known exception (10% early distribution penalty applies). A code of "2" indicates an early distribution exception applies (no 10% early distribution penalty). A NYCDCP participant who takes a distribution from the 401(k) or 401(a) should carefully review the 1099-R form and determine if the 10% early distribution does or does not apply for their situation. If the participant determines that the age 50 rule exception should apply, IRS Form 5329 (Additional Taxes on Qualified Plans (including IRAs) and Other Tax-Favored Accounts) will need to be prepared. In general, Part 1 of the form will be the only section that is required. Taxpayers who self-prepare their tax return should review IRS form 5329 instructions to ensure it is correctly reported. For taxpayers who use the services of a tax preparer, inform the tax preparer that you are eligible for the exception.

Taxation of SS Retirement Benefit

For most recent NYPD Service retirees, 85% of the Social Security Retirement benefits received will be federally taxable. The good news is that Social Security Retirement benefits are not currently taxed by NYS/NYC.

Pension Contributions (414H) Tax Issues

Under current law, both the regular and the ITHP member contributions to the NYCPPF are federally tax-deferred but are taxed at the NYS/NYC level.

NYC 1127 Payments

Once retired, the NYPD member is no longer subject to the 1127 section of the NYC Charter. The NYC 1127 payments apply to certain active members who reside outside of NYC and are considered a condition of employment, not a tax.

Distribution Planning

Many NYPD retirees incorrectly assume that the NYCDCP 457(b) is the most tax favorable retirement plan to receive distributions. It is not uncommon for an NYPD retiree to have multiple retirement plans (457(b), 401(k), 401(a), etc.) available for distribution. Every retiree should follow these five steps prior to taking a distribution from a retirement plan or IRA.

1. Determine if you need the money. Are there other sources available to get the money from (home equity loan, relative, college loans, etc.)? Also, review tax implications of withdrawing money from non-retirement accounts (brokerage account, 529 plan, etc.), if available.
2. Determine which retirement plan or IRA to take the money from. NYPD retirees may have multiple retirement plans to choose from. The tax implications are **not** the same for all retirement plans.
3. Determine if it is more tax efficient and possible to transfer (roll over) one retirement plan to another before taking a distribution. Also, determine if it is possible to isolate non-taxable money to avoid taxation.
4. Estimate the tax liability of the distribution at both the federal **and** state level. Many retirees fail to do this and are surprised how much tax is owed when their tax return is prepared.
5. Before submitting the distribution form, double check for accuracy. You want to avoid a costly tax mistake because you filled out the form incorrectly.

Distribution Planning-Creating Your Own "Pension Plan"

In the author's opinion, an excellent method to use when taking distributions from a retirement plan is to set-up recurring distributions. These recurring distributions provide structure to the retiree's monthly income and if done correctly can be tax efficient. The following is an example of a retiree who has set-up recurring distributions.

Assumptions
- 60-year-old NYPD retiree
- NYS resident
- Annual pension = $50,000
- NYCDCP 457(b) balance = $300,000
- Retiree has no other retirement plans

Author's Tip

For help with these create your own "pension plan" calculations use the Tax & RP App iPhone app. The app has three scenario calculators.

The retiree has decided to receive distributions from the NYCDCP 457(b) over a 30-year period and does not want any money remaining in the account at age 90 if he is still alive. Using a 2.5% rate of return factor, the retiree calculates he can receive $1,185.36 per month for the next 30 years. The monthly NYCDCP 457(b) distributions would be taxed at the federal level but will not be taxed at the NYS level due to the NYS Pension and Annuity exclusion. Alternatively, the retiree could calculate how many years his NYCDCP 457(b) will last based on a rate of return and a distribution amount. For example, assume the retiree desires a $20,000 annual distribution from the NYCDCP 457(b) plan. Using a 2% rate of return factor, the retiree calculates he can receive the $20,000 annual payments for approximately 18 years. After the 18 years of $20,000 distributions, the NYCDCP 457(b) balance is zero.

Required Minimum Distributions

Generally, the IRS requires taxpayers to begin receiving distributions from most retirement plans by April 1st of the calendar year following the year which the taxpayer reaches the age of 70 ½. The overall purpose of required minimum distributions (RMDs) is to ensure that taxpayers do not just accumulate wealth in retirement accounts and leave the funds untaxed to a beneficiary(ies). Essentially, RMDs force taxpayers to remove some money from retirement accounts as taxable distributions. For some taxpayers, including retired NYPD members, RMDs can cause a significant change to a taxpayer's tax burden at both the federal and state level. For the most part, RMD rules are simple to comply with, but in some instances can become complex. The following are some highlights of RMD rules.

Chapter 8: Taxes, Distribution Planning, & RMDs

- The federal government requires taxpayers to <u>annually</u> withdraw an amount from IRAs and/or employer sponsored retirement plans even if the taxpayer does not "need" the money.
- Distributions must be taken by April 1st of the calendar year following the year which the taxpayer reaches the age of 70 ½.
- A taxpayer can always withdraw more than the minimum amount, but if the taxpayer withdraws less than the required minimum a significant federal penalty may apply.
- RMD rules do <u>not</u> apply to Roth IRAs while the account owner is alive but do apply to Roth 401ks.
- Distributions are taxed at regular income tax rates.
- Failure to comply with RMD rules may result in an IRS imposed penalty of 50%.

The following is an example of a retired NYPD member, with significant retirement assets and who is subject to RMD rules.

Assumptions
- Retired NYPD member with a birthdate of 04/01/1949
- Rollover IRA (final withdrawal & VSF DROP) account balance = $425,000 as of 12/31/2018
- NYCDCP 457(b) account balance = $350,000 as of 12/31/2018
- Union Annuity Plan balance = $100,000 as of 12/31/2018
- Regular IRA account balance = $25,000 as of 12/31/2018
- Calculation
- Retired member will be 70 years old on 04/01/2019
- Retired member will be 70 ½ years old on 10/01/2019
- 2019 RMD must be distributed on or before 04/01/20, this date is referred to as the required beginning date
- 2020 RMD must be distributed by 12/31/2020
- Minimum distribution factor used for 2019 is 27.4
- Rollover IRA 2019 RMD = $15,511
- NYC DCP 457(b) 2019 RMD = $12,774
- Union Annuity Plan 2019 RMD = $3,650
- Regular IRA 2019 RMD = $912
- Total 2019 RMD = $32,847

The total 2019 RMD of $32,847 is added to the NYPD retiree's income for the year. As reviewed earlier, the original owner of a Roth IRA is not subject to RMDs, therefore making the Roth IRA a very attractive tax efficient retirement plan.

Required Minimum Distributions-Uniform Lifetime Table

Table #53 is the more common table used for RMDs. In general, this table is used for unmarried taxpayers, married taxpayers whose spouses are <u>not</u> more than ten years younger, and married taxpayers whose spouses are not the sole beneficiary of the retirement plan/IRA. To calculate the RMD, the taxpayer will need to know the account balance of the retirement plan/IRA as of 12/31 of the preceding year. The 12/31 balance will be divided by the divisor factor based on the taxpayer's age.

TABLE #53
RMDs-Uniform Lifetime Table

Age	Divisor	Age	Divisor	Age	Divisor
70	27.4	86	14.1	102	5.5
71	26.5	87	13.4	103	5.2
72	25.6	88	12.7	104	4.9
73	24.7	89	12.0	105	4.5
74	23.8	90	11.4	106	4.2
75	22.9	91	10.8	107	3.9
76	22.0	92	10.2	108	3.7
77	21.2	93	9.6	109	3.4
78	20.3	94	9.1	110	3.1
79	19.5	95	8.6	111	2.9
80	18.7	96	8.1	112	2.6
81	17.9	97	7.6	113	2.4
82	17.1	98	7.1	114	2.1
83	16.3	99	6.7	115+	1.9
84	15.5	100	6.3		
85	14.8	101	5.9		

Audits

Occasionally, active and retired NYPD members receive audit notices from the IRS and/or NYS. In many cases, the IRS audits are known as correspondence audits (CP2000) which means the matter can generally be resolved through the mail. Usually, a taxpayer receives a correspondence audit when the IRS computers do not match what was entered on the taxpayer's income tax return. If you receive a correspondence audit you should be guided by the following.

- Do not ignore the notice.
- Obtain the tax records for the year in question. If you do not have a copy of the tax return or are unable to obtain from your tax preparer request a "Tax Return Transcript" and a "Tax Account Transcript" (if applicable) from the IRS.
- Do not ignore the due date on the letter received by the IRS. If you are not able to meet the deadline; request an extension. The difficulty in requesting an extension is trying to get to speak to an actual person at the IRS (you may be on hold for an extended period).
- Compare the letter received by the IRS with your tax return and determine what generated the notice.
- If you disagree with the IRS's findings, prepare a response and provide supporting documentation if needed.

NYS Audits

Audits issued by the NYS Department of Taxation & Finance (NYSDTF) can often be quite challenging for taxpayers. A common audit that active NYPD members may receive is the failure to include NYCPPF member pension contributions on the NYS tax return. As previously reviewed, the member pension contributions made to the NYCPPF are subject to NYS/NYC taxes. If the taxpayer or tax preparer failed to include the pension contributions as taxable to NYS, the taxpayer will be required to pay the outstanding tax bill.

NYSDTF also audits distributions from retirement plans. Before agreeing to pay the requested taxes, the taxpayer should fully understand NYS tax law regarding distributions from the NYCDCP Special 401(k), Union Annuity Plans, the Pension & Annuity Exclusion, etc. In some cases, it may be cost effective to have a tax professional review the audit notice to determine if you are liable for the taxes.

Summary

This chapter reviewed the different types of certifications in the tax preparation industry and the importance of selecting a qualified and knowledgeable tax preparer. Many of the unique tax issues that apply to NYPD members were also reviewed. Understanding tax withholding on pension payments is a critical area of retirement planning that both pre and post retirees should understand. Nothing worse at tax time when an individual did not withhold enough federal taxes from their NYPD pension and now owes money.

Unfortunately, for many NYPD retirees' taxes are a significant detriment to a comfortable retirement. By using some of the strategies presented in this book, specifically the Roth IRA, the NYPD retiree may be able to limit the damaging effects of taxes during retirement years.

CHAPTER 9
Advanced Tax & Retirement Planning

This chapter will review more advanced tax and retirement planning strategies for active and retired NYPD members. Tax planning can be defined as an exercise undertaken to minimize tax liability through the best use of all available allowances, deductions, exclusions, exemptions, distribution/conversion strategies, etc. In general, tax planning is not undertaken when an individual prepares his or her tax return, due to the fact the tax year is already over, but rather is implemented **during** the tax year.

It should be noted that the material presented may or may not be suitable for everyone. Additionally, these strategies may require the services of a knowledgeable tax professional to ensure compliance with various tax laws. The following strategies will be reviewed:

- In-plan rollovers to designated Roth accounts
- Series of Substantial Equal Periodic Payments (SSEPP)
- "Back-door" Roth IRA
- 0% Capital Gains Tax
- Qualified Charitable Distribution
- Loans from retirement plans for retirees

There are also basic and complex tax planning strategies available for ADR retirees. Before making any tax or retirement planning decision, all ADR retirees should determine if there is a strategy available to pay less federal and state tax.

In-Plan Rollovers to Designated Roth Accounts

The Small Business Jobs Act of 2010 established in-plan rollovers to designated Roth accounts. This law permits (not required) plan sponsors that already had Roth 457(b), Roth 401(k), and Roth 403(b) to offer their participants an in-plan Roth conversion. This feature allows participants to roll over their pre-tax eligible retirement plans directly to the Roth designated account within the same plan. For example, a 457(b)-plan participant is permitted to directly roll over his or her 457(b) funds into a Roth 457(b) account of the same plan. Rolling over the funds from the 457(b) to the Roth 457(b) plan is a taxable event, and the amount rolled over is treated as ordinary income. A disadvantage of the law was that a participant had to be eligible for distribution under both the terms of the plan and by the Internal Revenue Code.

The requirement that the participant had to be eligible for a distribution was eliminated by the American Taxpayer Relief Act of 2012. It took the NYCDCP a few years before participants were able to take advantage of the new law, but in 2015 it became available for active NYCDCP participants. Once the eligible for a distribution requirement was eliminated, interesting tax and retirement planning strategies became available. For example, there may be times during an active NYPD member's career that they do not work for an entire year, such as due to a leave of absence (child care), injury at work, etc. During these non-work periods, it may be an opportune time to implement an in-plan rollover to a designated Roth account. The following is an example of this strategy.

Assumptions
- John is a 30-year-old active NYPD employee
- John's NYCDCP 457(b) balance = $125,000
- Married filing joint status and spouse, Mary, works in the private sector
- John's pre-tax salary = $100,000
- John's NYCPPF pre-tax contribution = $7,500
- Mary's pre-tax salary = $150,000
- Reside in NYS/NYC

Chapter 9: Advanced Tax & Retirement Planning

John and Mary both contribute, on a pre-tax basis, the maximum permitted to each of their employer's retirement plans. The NYCDCP offers both a 457(b) plan and a Roth 457(b) plan and permits participants to do in-plan Roth rollovers.

Mary has decided to take an unpaid leave of absence on January 1 for one year to care for their newborn child. Since Mary will not be working, John and Mary's income for the one-year period will be significantly reduced. The lower income may be an excellent time for John and Mary to do an in-plan Roth rollover. Table #54 compares John and Mary's 2018 federal taxes vs. 2019 federal taxes.

TABLE #54
In-Plan Rollover

Item	2018 Tax Year	2019 Tax Year
Total Gross Wages	$250,000	$100,000
Pre-tax Contributions	-$43,500	-$26,500
In-plan Rollover	N/A	$25,000
Adjusted Gross Income	$206,500	$98,500
Standard Deduction	-$24,000	-$24,400
Taxable Income	$182,500	$74,100
Federal Tax	$32,379	$8,504
Tax Bracket	24%	12%

Reviewing table #54 indicates that the $25,000 NYCDCP 457(b) to NYCDCP Roth 457(b) in-plan rollover was federally taxed at the low rate of 12%. John will receive an IRS form 1099-R from the NYCDCP reporting to the IRS that he directly rolled over the $25,000 to his Roth 457(b) plan. To avoid an underpayment penalty, John & Mary may need to send money to both the IRS & NYS. A disadvantage of the in-plan rollover for John & Mary is that the $25,000 is taxable by NYS/NYC.

Author's Tip

Taxpayers are not permitted to recharacterize in-plan rollovers to designated Roth accounts. Once the funds are designated Roth (converted), there is no going back to the non-Roth account, even if the assets of the Roth have decreased in value.

Series of Substantial Equal Periodic Payments (SSEPP)

The series of substantial equal periodic payment strategy also commonly referred to as the 72(t) election [IRC §72(t)(2)(a4)(iv)], is an IRS provision that permits taxpayers to remove funds from a retirement plan and not be subject to the 10% early distribution penalty regardless of the taxpayer's age. As reviewed earlier, distributions from most retirement plans are subject to the 10% early distribution penalty if the taxpayer is less than 59 ½ years old. By electing the 72(t) election and complying with the rules, the taxpayer avoids the 10% early distribution penalty. Currently, there are three methods available when electing the 72(t) exception: minimum distribution, fixed amortization, and fixed annuitization. Under the rules of the 72(t) election, the taxpayer does not arbitrarily decide how much money to withdraw. Instead, the taxpayer needs to perform calculations in order to determine how much can be withdrawn under the three available methods.

Once the calculations are performed, the taxpayer would select one of the three available methods. Generally, once one of the methods is selected, the taxpayer will be required to continue using the same method for a certain number of years.

> **Author's Tip**
>
> A retired NYPD member does not need to elect a 72(t) election for the NYCDCP 457(b) since there is no 10% early distribution penalty regardless of age. Additionally, retired NYPD members who can take advantage of the age 50 rule may not need the 72(t) election.

Retired NYPD Member Utilizing SSEPP-72(t) Example

The following is an example of a retired NYPD member using the 72(t) election in order to access funds prior to 59 ½ years old.

Assumptions
- 48 years old at retirement from NYPD
- 25 years of service
- Distribution interest rate of 3.65%
- Elected final withdrawal of $200,000 and rolled over to NYCDCP Special 401(k)
- Rolled over VSF DROP funds of $60,000 to NYCDCP Special 401(k)
- Rolled over Union Annuity Plan of $40,000 to NYCDCP Special 401(k)
- After completing the rollovers, the value of the NYCDCP Special 401(k) is $300,000
- Begins 72(t) election at 50 years old and the value of the NYCDCP Special 401(k) is $320,000

Chapter 9: Advanced Tax & Retirement Planning

VSF DROP $60,000

Union Annuity Plan $40,000

NYCDCP Special 401k
$200,000
+$60,000
+$40,000
=$300,000

Final Withdrawal $200,000

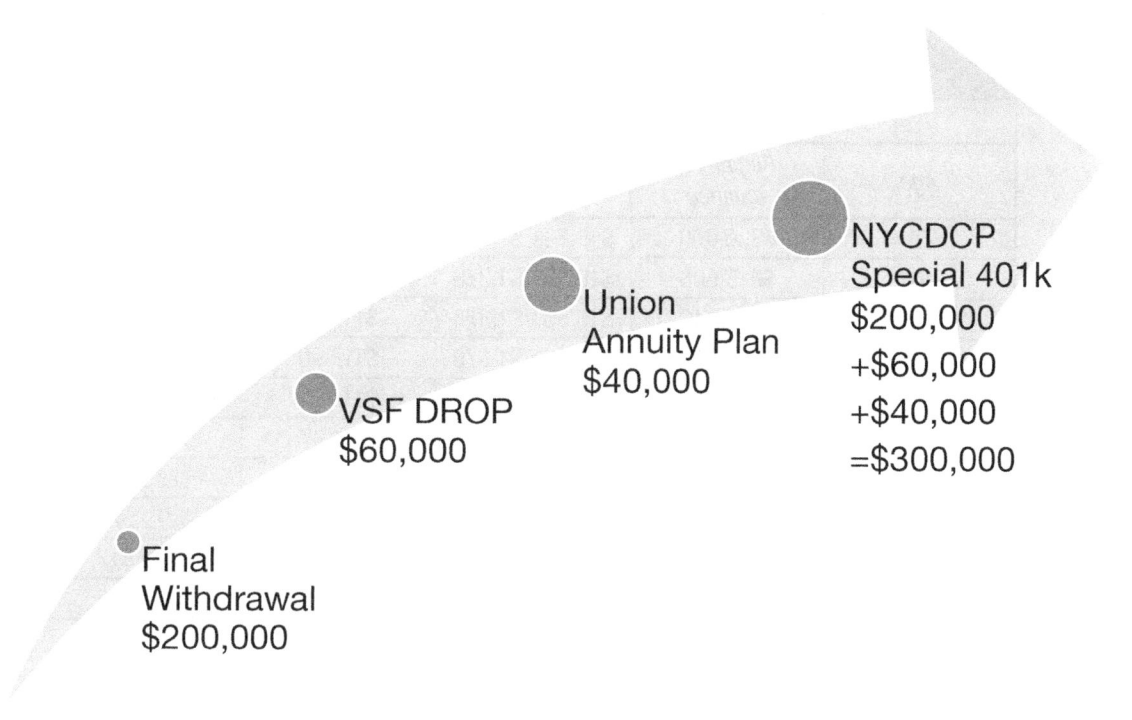

After the rollovers, the retired NYPD member has $300,000 available in the NYCDCP Special 401(k) plan for the 72(t) election.

Assume the NYPD retiree decides to perform a 72(t) election at age 50 when the value of the NYCDCP Special 401(k) plan is $320,000. Using the assumptions, the three methods can be calculated.

1. Minimum distribution = $9,357 per year or $780 per month
2. Fixed amortization = $16,531 per year or $1,378 per month
3. Fixed annuitization = $16,436 per year or $1,370 per month

Table #55 displays the results of the 72(t)-election based on the fixed amortization method for the NYPD retiree.

TABLE #55

72(t) Election-Fixed Amortization Method

Age	Beginning Balance	Distribution Year/month	Appreciation 4%	Ending Balance
50	$320,000	$16,531/$1,378	$12,139	$315,608
51	$315,608	$16,531/$1,378	$11,963	$311,040
52	$311,040	$16,531/$1,378	$11,780	$306,289
53	$306,289	$16,531/$1,378	$11,590	$301,348
54	$301,348	$16,531/$1,378	$11,393	$296,210
55	$296,210	$16,531/$1,378	$11,187	$290,866
56	$290,866	$16,531/$1,378	$10,973	$285,308
57	$285,308	$16,531/$1,378	$10,751	$279,528
58	$279,528	$16,531/$1,378	$10,520	$273,517
59	$273,517	$16,531/$1,378	$10,279	$267,265

In this example, the NYPD retiree will be required to distribute $16,531 per year or $1,378 per month until 59 ½ years old. Once the retiree reaches 59 ½ years old, the 72(t) rules were complied with and the retiree can change or stop the distribution amount. Analyzing the table, the retiree was able to distribute a total of $165,310 from age 50 to age 60 without incurring the 10% early distribution penalty.

Using a different appreciation rate changes the result of the ending balance. Using the previous assumptions, table #56 displays the results using a 2.5% appreciation rate.

TABLE #56

72(t) Election-Fixed Amortization Method (2.5%)

Age	Beginning Balance	Distribution Year/month	Appreciation 2.5%	Ending Balance
50	$320,000	$16,531/$1,378	$7,587	$311,056
51	$311,056	$16,531/$1,378	$7,363	$301,888
52	$301,888	$16,531/$1,378	$7,134	$292,491
53	$292,491	$16,531/$1,378	$6,899	$282,859
54	$282,859	$16,531/$1,378	$6,658	$272,986
55	$272,986	$16,531/$1,378	$6,411	$262,867
56	$262,867	$16,531/$1,378	$6,158	$252,494
57	$252,494	$16,531/$1,378	$5,899	$241,862
58	$241,862	$16,531/$1,378	$5,633	$230,964
59	$230,964	$16,531/$1,378	$5,361	$219,794

An important 72(t) rule to remember is once the retiree elects to begin 72(t) distributions, the distributions must continue until age 59 ½ or for five years whichever is <u>later</u>. If the retiree were to change the distribution amount prior to 59 ½ years old, the retiree would be subject to IRS imposed interest and penalties. For example, if the retiree in the above example were to distribute $25,000 at age 55 the interest and penalties would apply to the $25,000 and all the distributions before age 55.

The minimum distribution method works differently than the other two. Table #57, using the same assumptions (2.5% appreciation) as the previous example, displays the result if the retiree were to select the minimum distribution method.

TABLE #57

72(t) Election-Minimum Distribution Method (2.5%)

Age	Beginning Balance	Distribution Year/month	Appreciation 2.5%	Ending Balance
50	$320,000	$9,357/$780	$7,766	$318,409
51	$318,409	$9,562/$797	$7,721	$316,569
52	$316,569	$9,801/$817	$7,669	$314,437
53	$314,437	$10,014/$834	$7,611	$312,034
54	$312,034	$10,231/$852	$7,545	$309,348
55	$309,348	$10,451/$871	$7,472	$306,370
56	$306,370	$10,675/$889	$7,392	$303,087
57	$303,087	$10,863/$905	$7,306	$299,529
58	$299,529	$11,094/$924	$7,211	$295,647
59	$295,647	$11,327/$944	$7,108	$291,427

Reviewing table #57, the retiree was able to slightly increase yearly/monthly distributions as he or she got older. The retiree received total distributions of $103,375 during the period and $291,427 remained at the completion of the 72(t) election

72(t) Election and Final Withdrawal vs. No Final Withdrawal

In many ways, the 72(t) election creates an interesting added twist to the decision-making process of whether to take the final withdrawal (final loan). Very often, NYPD pre-retirees do not select the final withdrawal because they have been incorrectly informed that the funds are not accessible until 59 ½ years old, unless an exception applies. The 72(t) election makes the final withdrawal funds available before 59 ½ years old without the 10% early distribution penalty if the rules are followed.

The following example will show how a NYPD retiree is able to take advantage of the 72(t) election to begin to make up a reduced pension due to selecting the final withdrawal.

Chapter 9: Advanced Tax & Retirement Planning

Assumptions
- 48 years old at retirement from NYPD
- 25 years of service
- Distribution interest rate of 3.65%
- Final withdrawal available = $200,000
- VSF DROP funds = $60,000
- Union Annuity Plan balance = $40,000

Table #58 displays the decision the NYPD pre-retiree is trying to make.

TABLE #58
72(t) Election Final Withdrawal vs. No Final Withdrawal

Item	No Final Withdrawal	Final Withdrawal
Annual Pension	$75,000	$58,113
Monthly Pension	$6,250	$4,843
Difference	$1,407 per month	

If the NYPD pre-retiree elects the final withdrawal, the monthly pension is reduced by $1,407 per month. Is there a tax efficient and penalty free method available for this pre-retiree to begin to make up the reduced pension? Yes, by utilizing the 72(t) election. Using the assumptions and the beginning balance of $300,000 the retiree would calculate the three 72(t) methods and select one of them. The following are the three calculated methods.

- Minimum distribution = $8,889 per year or $741 per month
- Fixed amortization = $16,113 per year or $1,343 per month
- Fixed annuitization = $15,993 per year or $1,333 per month

Assume the retiree selects the fixed amortization method and elects distributions monthly. By selecting this method, the retiree was able to lessen the effects of the reduced pension, establish ownership of the final withdrawal, has the opportunity to earn interest/appreciation on the final withdrawal, and provide for a beneficiary in the event of an early death.

TABLE #59
72(t) Election Final Withdrawal vs. No Final Withdrawal

Item	No Final Withdrawal	Final Withdrawal
Annual Pension	$75,000	$58,113
Monthly Pension	$6,250	$4,843
72(t) Election	N/A	$1,343
Total Monthly	$6,250	$6,186
Difference	$64 per month	

72(t) Election and a Significant Final Withdrawal Amount

The 72(t) election may be an effective retirement funding mechanism for the NYPD member who has a substantial final withdrawal amount, retires in his or her early fifties and does not rollover the funds to a governmental retirement plan. By electing the 72(t) election it allows the retiree to take the full final withdrawal and only be subject to the rules of the 72(t) election for a fairly short period of time. The following is an example of a 54-year-old retiring NYPD member with a significant final withdrawal.

Assumptions
- 54 years old at retirement from NYPD and retiree did not want to rollover funds to any governmental plan
- 30 years of service
- Distribution interest rate of 3.65%
- Final withdrawal available of $415,000
- VSF DROP funds of $110,000
- Union Annuity Plan balance of $75,000

The retiree combines the $415,000 final withdrawal, the $110,000 VSF DROP, and the $75,000 Union Annuity Plan into an IRA. Once all the rollovers are complete, the NYPD retiree would have $600,000 available for the 72(t) election. Next, the NYPD retiree would need to calculate the three 72(t) methods and select one of them. The following are the three calculated methods based on the assumptions.

- Minimum distribution = $19,672 per year or $1,639 per month
- Fixed amortization = $32,936 per year or $2,745 per month
- Fixed annuitization = $32,765 per year or $2,730 per month

Table #60 displays the result of the 54-year-old retiree electing the fixed amortization method at age 55 when the balance of the IRA is $615,000. As the table indicates, the 72(t) election would only be in effect for a short period of time and after the five-year period the retiree would be permitted to change the dollar amount of the distribution or could even stop distributions if he or she wished.

TABLE #60

72(t) Election Significant Final Withdrawal

Age	Beginning Balance	Distribution Year/month	Appreciation 2.5%	Ending Balance
55	$615,000	$32,936/$2,745	$14,552	$596,616
56	$596,616	$32,936/$2,745	$14,092	$577,772
57	$577,772	$32,936/$2,745	$13,621	$558,457
58	$558,457	$32,936/$2,745	$13,138	$538,659
59	$538,659	$32,936/$2,745	$12,463	$518,186

Final Word about the 72(t) Election

The 72(t) election is not for everyone. The retiree needs to fully understand how the provision works and determine if it is the best course of action to take. If the 72(t) election is not implemented correctly or is modified, the retiree will more than likely be subject to IRS imposed penalties and interest.

"Back-door" Roth IRA

The back-door Roth IRA is a strategy used by some taxpayers whose earnings are greater than the Roth IRA threshold limits. For example, if a single taxpayer has income of $150,000, contributions to a Roth IRA generally are not permitted. The back-door Roth IRA is a tax planning method that "gets around" the income threshold limits. The level of difficulty implementing this strategy is based on different factors and may not be suitable for some taxpayers. Implementing a back-door Roth IRA strategy incorrectly often results in unfavorable tax consequences.

The first step in implementing a back-door Roth strategy is determining whether the taxpayer is eligible to contribute to an IRA. To contribute to an IRA, the taxpayer must generally have earned income and must be less than 70½ years old. If the taxpayer fails to meet the earned income test and the age test, a contribution to an IRA is not permitted. If an IRA contribution is not permitted, the taxpayer cannot do a back-door Roth IRA. The second step is to determine if the taxpayer is eligible for a deductible IRA. The third step is whether the taxpayer already has an IRA. If the taxpayer is not eligible for a deductible IRA and does not currently have an IRA, the process is straightforward.

For example, assume an active NYPD member is 55-years-old and a single taxpayer. Also, the active NYPD member has earnings above the threshold to make a deductible IRA, has earned income above the Roth IRA threshold, and does not currently have an IRA. Under these assumptions, the taxpayer could contribute $7,000 to a non-deductible IRA. Since the taxpayer did not receive an IRA deduction, the funds contributed to the IRA were made with after-tax funds. At some point after the non-deductible IRA contribution is made, the taxpayer converts the IRA to a Roth IRA. The original $7,000 is not subject to tax, but any earnings that were made prior to the conversion are subject to taxation.

If a taxpayer currently has an IRA that contains after-tax money, the back-door Roth IRA strategy is more involved. To implement the strategy, the taxpayer will need to isolate the after-tax money in the IRA, if possible. Another complication of the back-door Roth strategy is if the taxpayer has a before-tax IRA and makes a non-deductible (after-tax) contribution to an

IRA. For example, assume a taxpayer has a $45,000 traditional IRA that contains all pre-tax money. If the taxpayer makes a non-deductible (after-tax) contribution to an IRA, the total IRA balance is $50,000. Due to the pro-rata rule, if the taxpayer takes a distribution, including a Roth conversion, 5% of the distribution will be non-taxable. If the taxpayer decided to convert $5,000 from the IRA to a Roth IRA after making the non-deductible contribution, only $250 would be non-taxable, while the remaining $4,750 would be taxable.

0% Capital Gains Tax

This strategy can be complicated and requires the taxpayer to understand the difference between ordinary income tax rates and capital gains tax rates. Under current law, long-term capital gains are taxed at 0% if the taxpayer(s) is in the 10% or 12% ordinary income tax brackets. The following is an example of this strategy using the following assumptions.

Assumptions
- 55-year-old NYPD retiree
- Married filing joint status and spouse does not work
- NYCPPF pension = $50,000
- Pension federal tax withholding = $5,000
- Dividend income = $3,500
- Value of IBM stock = $100,000
- Basis of IBM stock = $20,000

The NYPD retiree and spouse would like to sell the IBM stock, but they don't want to pay any federal capital gains tax. They have owned the stock for years and have a gain of $80,000 ($100,000 - $20,000 basis). After reviewing their overall tax situation, the federal income tax brackets, and the capital gain tax rules, the couple decides to sell $50,000 of the IBM stock. On their federal tax return, they report $3,500 of dividend income, $40,000 capital gain ($50,000 - $10,000 basis), and the $50,000 pension. The couple has adjusted gross income of $93,500. After taking the 2018 standard deduction of $24,000, their taxable income is $69,500. To correctly calculate the federal tax due, the couple will need to complete the IRS Qualified

Dividends and Capital Gain Tax Worksheet. After completing the worksheet, it is determined that both the dividends and the entire $40,000 capital gain is taxed at 0%.

Qualified Charitable Distribution

A Qualified Charitable Distribution (QSD) is a tax planning strategy that permits certain taxpayers to remove funds from an IRA tax-free if the funds are sent directly to a public charity. Obviously, the taxpayer needs to be charitably inclined, but with diligent tax planning, the taxpayer may also benefit. This strategy may also work well in combination with other strategies presented in this chapter. The following are the requirements for a QSD.

- Taxpayer must be at least 70½ years old on the date of the distribution
- Maximum distribution is $100,000 per taxpayer
- In general, distribution comes from the taxpayer's IRA
- A QCD is not permitted from retirement plans (457(b), 401(k), etc.)
- A Roth IRA could also be used, but that is not relevant, because Roth IRA distributions are non-taxable
- An inherited IRA could be used if the beneficiary is at least 70½ years old on the date of the distribution
- The distribution must go **directly** to a public charity (no private foundations, donor-advised fund, etc.)

The following is an example of a married filing joint 72-year-old NYPD retiree using the QCD strategy. Assume the retiree is required to take a required minimum distribution of $15,625 from his $400,000 IRA balance, receives a $40,000 annual NYCPPF pension, and a $24,000 Social Security retirement benefit. The taxpayers do not need the distribution and would prefer to send the distribution to their favorite public charity. Table #61 (tax year 2018) compares claiming the distribution as taxable vs. sending the distribution (non-taxable) to a public charity.

TABLE #61
QCD Strategy

Item	Taxable	Non-Taxable
IRA Distribution	$15,625	$0
Pension	$40,000	$40,000
Taxable Portion of SS	$20,400	$12,800
Adjusted Gross Income	$76,025	$52,800
Standard Deduction	-$26,600	-$26,600
Taxable Income	$49,425	$26,200
Tax	$5.,550	$2,766

By implementing the QCD strategy, the taxpayers significantly reduced the taxable portion of their Social Security benefit, achieved tax savings of $2,784, and helped their favorite charity.

Loans from Retirement Plans for Retirees

Active NYPD employees can borrow money from their NYCDCP retirement plans (457(b) & 401(k) plans). Another option for the active member is to borrow money from the NYCPPF. If the active NYPD employee follows the IRS rules regarding loans, there is no tax consequence. Unfortunately, retired NYPD members are not permitted to take a loan from their NYCDCP account or from the NYCPPF. In general, if the retiree needs funds from a retirement plan, a distribution is made. In most cases, once a distribution occurs, the retiree is subject to taxes and possibly a penalty.

Is there a strategy available for a NYPD retiree to take a loan from a retirement plan? Yes. Very simply, a retiree that has his or her own business could transfer funds from the NYCDCP 457(b) or 401(k) to their business 401(k) plan. Once the funds are in the business 401(k), the retiree could take a loan if the custodian and plan document permits, or a retiree could establish a new business and create a Solo 401(k) plan.

For example, a NYPD retiree has decided to start her own catering business. The retiree has a sizable NYCDCP 457(b) account, but she does not want to take a distribution due to the tax consequences. The retiree has determined that she needs at least $30,000 to start up the business and is confident that it will be successful. After forming the business (LLC, S Corp,

Sole-Proprietor, etc.), the retiree opens a Solo 401(k) with a custodian that offers a loan feature. After the Solo 401(k) is established, the retiree transfers $75,000 from her 457(b) account into her Solo 401(k) plan. Once the funds are in the Solo 401(k) plan, the retiree can take a loan to fund her new business.

Tax Planning and the Accidental Disability Retiree

A NYPD member who retires with an Accidental Disability Retirement (ADR) pension, also referred to as 3/4s, may have the opportunity to perform tax planning to achieve lower taxes at both the federal and state level.

A NYPD retiree that receives an ADR pension should understand that this type of pension benefit is unique, and tax planning opportunities may be available that the Service retiree may not be able to take advantage of. There are many different tax and retirement planning strategies available; some are basic, while others are more complex. Every tax and retirement planning decision of an ADR retiree should be carefully reviewed.

A NYPD pre-retiree who is anticipating or has been approved an ADR pension should fully understand the non-taxable and taxable portion of his or her pension. The decision to remove pension contributions (final withdrawal) is critical to understand because the result will ultimately determine the level of tax planning that will be available.

The following are some examples of tax and retirement planning strategies that the author has provided to ADR retirees.

- Non-taxable distribution from a retirement plan
- Retirement plan conversions to a Roth IRA
- Roth IRA conversions and state taxes
- Deductible IRA
- Aggressive retirement plan contributions
- Earned Income Credit
- Non-taxable Social Security Retirement or Disability benefit
- Married Filing Joint vs. Married Filing Separate
- 0% Capital Gains Tax
- World Trade Center - 9/11
- Tax-efficient investing outside of retirement plans

Summary

This chapter reviewed a few advanced retirement planning topics that may not be suitable for everyone. In-plan rollovers to the NYCDCP Roth 457(b) or 401(k) is a new retirement planning strategy that some members should consider. The election of the 72(t) is a useful retirement income strategy but should only be used after a complete understanding of the various rules and methods. The 72(t) election is somewhat restrictive since once it is elected; the individual is not able to modify (in most cases) the payment plan without incurring significant IRS imposed penalties and interest.

Active and retired NYPD members who have a taxable brokerage account should review the 0% capital gains tax strategy. Retirees subject to RMDs and who are charitably inclined, may want to consider Qualified Charitable Distributions (QCDs). Finally, ADR retirees should be aware of favorable tax planning opportunities that may be available for their unique situation.

CHAPTER 10

Who to Turn to for Advice

Active NYPD members and retirees are often bombarded with financial information from many sources. These sources may include the internet, newspapers, magazines, unions, seminars, the "expert" at work, etc. This information or "advice" may be overwhelming, inaccurate, and confusing at times. Sometimes it appears that everyone has a theory or opinion on how to retire or how to invest money. If an active NYPD member or retiree decides to seek help from a financial planner, financial advisor, tax preparer, insurance salesperson etc. here are a few basic guidelines to keep in mind.

- Always remember this is your hard-earned money
- Ask questions
- Thoroughly understand any financial product(s) you are considering purchasing
- Do not be pressured into buying any financial product without a complete understanding of the fees, commissions, restrictions, tax implications, etc.
- Nothing is free

Ten Basic Questions to Ask a Financial Planner/Advisor

1. What experience do you have?
2. What are your qualifications/credentials?
3. What services do you offer?
4. What is your approach to financial planning?
    - type of clients
    - viewpoint on investing

5. Will you be the only person working with me?
6. How will I pay for your services?
7. How much do you typically charge?
8. Could anyone besides me benefit from your recommendations?
9. Have you ever been publicly disciplined for any unlawful or unethical actions in your professional career?
10. Can I have it in writing?
    - a written agreement that details the services to be provided

Five Specific Questions to Ask a Tax Preparer/Advisor

1. Do you know what Series of Substantial Equal Periodic Payments (72t election) means?
2. Do you know which type of retirement plans the final withdrawal can be rolled into?
3. What are the federal and NYS tax consequences of not rolling over the taxable portion of the final withdrawal?
4. At retirement, should I rollover my NYCDCP 457(b) account to an IRA?
5. At retirement, should I rollover my Union Annuity Plan to an IRA?

Credentials

The "alphabet soup" of the various credentials in the financial planning/advice area is mind boggling. For some consumers, it may be very difficult to sort through all of them and decide. Of course, having a credential should not be the sole reason in choosing an individual to help with your finances, but it is usually a good place to start your search. The following credentials are the better-known ones.

Certified Financial Planner® (CFP)

At a minimum, a CFP® has successfully completed the following coursework.

- General principles of financial planning
- Insurance planning
- Employee benefits planning
- Investment planning
- Income tax planning

- Retirement planning
- Estate planning

A CFP® professional has also met the following requirements.

- Examination: a comprehensive exam covering over 100 financial planning topics.
- Experience: 6,000 hours of experience based on the Standard Pathway or 4,000 hours based on the Apprenticeship Pathway.
- Ethics: Code of Ethics and other requirements are to be followed.
- Education: a bachelor's degree (or higher) and at least 30 hours of continuing education every two years.

Enrolled Agent

An Enrolled Agent (EA) is a tax practitioner license granted by the U.S. Department of Treasury. The IRS refers to the enrolled agent as an elite status and is the highest credential the IRS awards. EAs' specialize in areas of taxation and are authorized to represent taxpayers before all administrative levels of the Internal Revenue Service in reference to audits, appeals, and collections. Only Enrolled Agents, CPAs, and attorneys may represent taxpayers before the IRS. The EA license is granted after the successful completion of exams or in some instances after 5 years of relevant work experience at the IRS.

Chartered Financial Consultant

The Chartered Financial Consultant (ChFC) is a financial planning designation granted by the American College in Pennsylvania. The following are the requirements of a ChFC.

- Completed a comprehensive curriculum in financial planning
- Passed a series of written examinations
- Has met specific experience requirements
- Maintains ethical standards

Chartered Life Underwriter

The Chartered Life Underwriter (CLU) is an insurance and financial planning designation granted by the American College in Pennsylvania. The requirements of the CLU are like the ChFC, but the CLU may be more familiar with insurance products.

Chartered Financial Analyst

A Chartered Financial Analyst (CFA) is a professional designation granted by the CFA Institute. Of all the various credentials, the CFA may be the most rigorous to achieve. In order to become a CFA, an individual would need to pass three levels of exams covering accounting, economics, ethics, money management, and security analysis. Additionally, there is a three-year work experience requirement and a bachelor's degree requirement.

Certified Public Accountant

The Certified Public Accountant (CPA) is a designation granted by the American Institute of Certified Public Accountants. CPA's have completed various education and experience requirements. CPA's work in many areas of business and may not specialize in taxation.

The CPA/PFS is a Certified Public Accountant with a Personal Financial Specialist (PFS) designation. This designation is granted to CPA's who have completed a level of financial planning work experience, passed a personal financial planning exam, and completed continuing education requirements.

Methods of Compensation

The different forms or methods of compensation paid to financial planners or advisors may also be confusing to the consumer. Prior to meeting with a prospective advisor, individuals should research and understand these different methods of compensation. The following are some common forms of compensation paid to financial advisors.

Fee-Only

A fee-only advisor is compensated solely by the client and does not accept commissions from selling insurance or investment products. The fee-only advisor may charge a set fee based on a specific project or charge a fee based on the amount of time spent working with a client.

Fee or asset-based

The fee or asset-based advisor is often confused with the fee-only advisor. An asset-based advisor charges a fee based on the amount of the assets under management. For example, a fee-based advisor may charge a yearly fee of 1.25% of the total value of a client's portfolio. For a $100,000 portfolio this yearly fee would be $1,250.

Commissions

An advisor who charges a commission is compensated based on the financial product that is sold to the client.

Fee-based and commissions

An advisor who charges a combination of fees and commissions. The fees charged may be for work done to develop financial planning recommendations and commissions are received from any products sold.

CHAPTER 11
Case Studies

Case Study #1 – Monthly Distributions

Case study #1 reviews a single person, Cathy, who has fully retired at an early age. The case study is presented to explain a tax-efficient withdrawal strategy from the NYCDCP 457(b) plan that has a significant balance.

Background

Cathy
- 48 years old
- Single with no dependents
- Resides in Florida
- Annual pension = $55,000
- 457(b) account balance = $475,000

Cathy worked for the NYPD for 25 years and consistently contributed to her NYCDCP 457(b) plan. Cathy only contributed her basic contributions to the NYCPPF during her career but did aggressively contribute to the NYCDCP 457(b) plan. Once Cathy retired from the NYPD, she sold her house, moved to Florida, and purchased a condominium overlooking the ocean. Cathy does not have a mortgage but does have a small monthly car payment. Cathy is very risk-averse and has her entire 457(b) balance in an investment option that she hopes will provide a 3% rate of return during her retirement years. Cathy has performed various calculations, based on life expectancy, to determine how much of her 457(b) account can be distributed annually as shown in table #62.

TABLE #62
Monthly Distributions

Life Expectancy Age	Annual 457(b) Distribution
80	$23,297
85	$21,428
90	$20,041
95	$18,981
100	$18,153

Cathy has decided to request recurring monthly distributions from her 457(b) account in the amount of $1,512.75 ($18,153 annualized). Due to the 20% federal tax withholding rule, Cathy will receive a monthly distribution check of $1,210.20. An advantage of the NYCDCP 457(b) plan is that Cathy is not subject to the 10% early distribution penalty even though she is less than 59 ½ years old. At retirement, Cathy completed an IRS W-4P form for her pension entering single with zero allowances. Based on Cathy's W-4P, approximately $602 (based on 2018) will be withheld for federal income tax from her monthly pension amount ($4,583.33). Cathy will have approximately $5,191 ($3,981 + 1,210) a month of after-tax money to meet her retirement needs. Based on tax year 2018 and Cathy claiming the standard deduction on her tax return, she would receive a federal tax refund of approximately $1,461. Cathy does not have any state income tax issues, because currently the state of Florida does not have an income tax system. By Cathy electing to distribute her 457(b) account over a 52-year period, she has in a sense created her own pension plan. Although Cathy is concerned about the erosion of her pension benefit and 457(b) account distributions due to inflation, she is hopeful that she will receive a Social Security Retirement benefit.

Chapter 11: Case Studies

Case Study #2 – Significant Pre-Tax Retirement Plan Balances

Case study #2 reviews a single person, Danny Deferral, who has recently retired at age 60 after working for the NYPD for 35 years and has significant pre-tax balances in his retirement plans. The case study is presented to review a retiree subject to a higher tax bracket in retirement than when working and decides to utilize a tax bracket management strategy.

Background

Danny
- 60 years old
- Single with no dependents
- Annual pension benefit = $90,000
- Social Security Retirement benefit at age 70 = $36,000 (85% taxable)
- NYCDCP 457(b) balance = $625,000
- NYCDCP 401(k) balance = $350,000
- Rollover IRA = $150,000

Danny has aggressively contributed to his NYCDCP 457(b) plan on a before-tax basis for most of his NYPD career. After contributing the maximum to his 457(b) plan, Danny also contributed to his NYCDCP 401(k) plan on a before-tax basis. At retirement, Danny elected to remove his excess pension contributions ($150,000) and roll over the funds into an IRA. Danny was able to contribute significant amounts to his retirement plans because he had very few expenses throughout his working career. Danny has occupied a house that is a two-family home owned by his parents and has never paid rent or a mortgage. The only expenses Danny pays are half of the real estate taxes for the two-family home, car insurance, and utilities for his half of the house. While working, Danny was very proud of his ability to defer taxes on his contributions to retirement plans and for many years was in the 15% tax bracket. If Danny does not perform some basic tax planning, he is going to have significant tax obligations when distributions are required from his retirement plans at age 70½. Table #63 displays the approximate appreciation (using a 4% rate of appreciation assumption) of Danny's retirement assets if he does not distribute any money over a 10-year period.

TABLE #63
Significant Pre-tax Balances

Retirement Asset	Appreciation After 10 Years
457(b) Plan	$925,153
401(k) Plan	$518,085
Rollover IRA	$222,037
Total	$1,665,275

Danny's first required minimum distribution (RMD) from his retirement plans would be approximately $60,777 ($33,765 from his 457(b), $18,908 from his 401(k), and $8,104 from his rollover IRA). The $60,777 RMD is treated as ordinary income, and when added to his yearly pension ($90,000) & Social Security benefit ($30,600), Danny will have gross income of approximately $181,377. Danny anticipates not being able to itemize deductions during his retirement years, so he will take the standard deduction. Danny estimates that his taxable income will place him in the 32% tax bracket.

Danny may want to consider performing Roth conversions during the 10-year period prior to his required beginning date. Danny has recently learned that Roth IRAs are not subject to RMDs, and he is hoping that will lessen some of his taxes as he gets older. Based on the federal tax brackets for a specific year, Danny should "fill up" a tax bracket with a Roth conversion. For example, Danny determines his tax year 2018 taxable income to be $78,000 based on a standard deduction of $12,000. Taxable income of $78,000 puts Danny in the 22% federal tax bracket. Danny decides to fill up the 22% tax bracket with a Roth conversion and then also convert some retirement assets at the 24% tax bracket.

After Danny reviews the 2018 federal income tax brackets, he determines that he can convert $4,500 at the 22% tax bracket and up to $75,000 at the 24% tax bracket. Danny's plan is to perform Roth conversions using the tax bracket management strategy for each year until he is subject to RMDs.

Chapter 11: Case Studies

Case Study #3 – Stay or Go?

Case study #3 reviews a retirement planning scenario based on a couple, John and Mary. The case study is presented to the reader to highlight the benefits of compounding interest, ongoing contributions to retirement plans, and delaying retirement from the NYPD.

Background

John
- 45 years old
- NYPD Sergeant
- 20 years of service
- Appointment date of July 1998
- Gross salary = $130,000
- Contributes 7.15% to the NYCPPF
- Contributes to the NYCDCP 457(b)

Mary
- 45 years old
- Registered nurse
- Employed at a hospital
- Gross salary = $75,000
- Contributes to a 403(b)
- Plans to retire at age 55

John and Mary were married in 1998, have two children (ages 14 & 12), and own a home on Long Island. When John & Mary got married, they did not have a lot of money saved. They were fortunate enough to be able to buy a home with help from Mary's grandmother. John is trying to decide if he should retire from the NYPD but doesn't think he has any professional skills that would be marketable outside of the NYPD. John still enjoys his job; but like any job, it can be stressful at times. As John and Mary's children get closer to college age, John is concerned about the uncertainty of a new job. He is considering working for the NYPD until age 55 so he can fully retire at the same time as his wife, Mary. Mary intends to continue with her nursing profession and has increased her hours since their children have gotten older. John and Mary have been able to consistently contribute to their retirement accounts due to both working and by living within their means. They have gotten accustomed to contributing to their retirement accounts and are confident that they will be able to continue to do so. John and Mary intend to provide some financial assistance to their children for them to attend a public college in New York State. They anticipate that their mortgage will be paid off by the time they are 57 years old. Once retired, they plan to do extensive traveling and volunteer work.

John's current assets
- NYCPPF ASF = $175,000
- NYCDCP 457(b) balance = $200,000
- Union Annuity Plan balance = $30,000

Mary's current assets
- 403(b) from hospital = $55,000
- Roth IRA = $8,000

John and Mary jointly owned current assets
- Stock brokerage account = $10,000
- Market value of home = $525,000

Children's college money (from grandparents)
- 529 Plan #1 = $15,000
- 529 Plan #2 = $12,000

John's Retirement Projections
- John has made estimated pension calculations and retirement projections based on 20 and 30 years of service to help decide if he should retire from the NYPD or not.

Retirement assumptions based on 20 years of service.
- Retire at age 45 from the NYPD
- NYCDCP 457(b) balance = $200,000
- Union Annuity Plan balance = $30,000
- VSF annual benefit of $12,000 once retired
- Annual pension of $55,800 (pre-tax) after taking final withdrawal
- Pension final withdrawal = $162,500

Calculations
- 20 Years of Service
- FAS = $130,000
- Required amount = $125,000
- ASF balance = $175,000
- Excess = $50,000
- 50% of FAS = $65,000
- Annuitized value of excess = $4,089
- Final withdrawal "cost" = $13,289
- Annual pension (pre-tax) = $55,800
- Monthly pension (pre-tax) = $4,650

Retirement assumptions based on 30 years of service.
- Retire at age 55 from the NYPD
- NYCDCP 457(b) balance = $450,000 (5% rate of return and contributions of $10,000 per year)
- Union Annuity Plan = $67,000
- VSF DROP = $120,000
- Annual pension of $93,080 (pre-tax) after taking final withdrawal
- Pension final withdrawal = $520,500

Calculations
- 30 Years of Service
- FAS = $150,000
- Estimated value of 60ths = $23,300
- Required amount = $125,000
- ASF balance = $533,000
- Excess = $408,000
- 50% of FAS = $75,000
- Annuitized value of excess = $38,254
- Estimated annuitized value of ITHP-NYC = $6,500
- Final withdrawal "cost" = $49,974
- Annual pension (pre-tax) = $93,080
- Monthly pension (pre-tax) = $7,757

Table #65 compares the 20-year retirement vs. the 30-year retirement.

TABLE #65		
20 Year vs. 30 Year		
Item	*20 Year Retirement*	*30 Year Retirement*
Annual pension	$55,800	$93,080
ASF balance	$175,000	$533,000
Final withdrawal	$162,500	$520,500
Annual VSF	$12,000	N/A
VSF DROP	N/A	$120,000
NYCDCP 457(b)	$200,000	$450,000
Union Annuity Plan	$30,000	$67,000

As table #65 indicates, John will be able to significantly increase his overall wealth and receive a pension that is 67% more at a 30-year retirement than a 20-year retirement. Retiring at 55 years old, John will have a few different options available to fund his retirement.

- Roll over his final withdrawal ($520,500), VSF DROP ($120,000), and Union Annuity Plan ($67,000) for a total of $707,500 into the NYCDCP Special 401(k).
- Roll over his final withdrawal ($520,500), VSF DROP ($120,000), and Union Annuity Plan ($67,000) for a total of $707,500 into a rollover IRA and elect 72(t) for a five-year period.

- Receive distributions from his NYC DCP 457(b) or Special 401(k) without the 10% early distribution penalty. Distributions will be subject to federal taxes and possibly state taxes.
- Live off his $93,080 annual pension benefit and allow his retirement accounts to appreciate.

If John decides to stay working for the NYPD until 55 years old, he may want to consider contributing to the NYCDCP Roth 457(b) plan instead of the 457(b) plan. Contributing to the Roth 457(b) plan will reduce some of his future tax liabilities.

Case Study #4 – Tax-Efficient Retirement Distributions

Case study #4 reviews a NYPD retiree implementing tax-efficient withdrawal strategies from various retirement plans.

Susan's Retirement Projections

Susan has decided to retire after 20 years of service and wants to fully retire and remain a NYS resident. She plans to fund her retirement using the following retirement assets.
- NYCPPF Pension
- VSF
- Yearly distributions from her NYCDCP Special 401(k) plan for ages 50 to 60
- Distributions from her NYCDCP 457(b) plan for ages 60 to 90
- Begin Social Security Retirement benefits at age 70

Retirement assumptions based on 20 years of service.
- Retirement & IRS age = 50
- NYCDCP 457(b) plan balance = $150,000
- Union Annuity Plan balance = $20,000
- Yearly pension benefit = $53,151 (before-tax) after taking final distribution
- Pension final withdrawal amount = $123,000

Calculations
- Years of service = 20
- Final average salary (FAS) = $125,000
- Required amount = $120,000
- ASF balance = $135,000
- Overage (excess) = $15,000
- 50% of FAS = $62,500
- Value of overage = $1,299
- Final distribution "cost" = $10,648
- Yearly pension benefit before-tax = $53,151
- Monthly pension benefit before-tax = $4,429

Chapter 11: Case Studies

At retirement, Susan decided to roll over the final withdrawal ($123,000) and the Union Annuity Plan ($20,000) into the NYCDCP Special 401(k) plan. For ages 50 through 60, Susan plans to receive distributions from her NYCDCP Special 401(k) account since there is no 10% early distribution penalty due to her retirement age of 50. Distributions from the Special 401(k) plan will also provide favorable NYS tax consequences. Susan will pay federal tax on the 401(k) distributions, but she will only pay minimal or possibly no NYS taxes due to the calculation she will perform each year. Susan plans to <u>not</u> take any distributions from her NYCDCP 457(b) plan and she assumes a 5% appreciation rate for 10 years. Susan will have the following retirement funds to use from age 50 to 60.

- $4,429 monthly pension benefit
- $1,500 monthly distribution from the NYCDCP Special 401(k) plan
- $12,000 annual VSF payment
    - Total annual gross income before-tax: $83,151
    - Total monthly gross income before-tax: $6,929

For ages 60 through 90, Susan plans to receive distributions from her NYCDCP 457(b) plan which has appreciated to $244,334. Susan will pay federal tax on the 457(b) distributions, but she will not have to pay NYS/NYC taxes, because she will take advantage of the $20,000 NYS Pension/Annuity Exclusion. Susan's 401(k) plan no longer has a balance since she used it from age 50 to 60. Susan will have the following retirement funds to use from age 60 to 70.

1. $4,429 monthly pension benefit
2. $1,275 monthly distribution from the NYCDCP 457(b) plan
3. $12,000 annual VSF payment
    - Total annual gross income pre-tax: $80,451
    - Total monthly gross income pre-tax: $6,704

Although Susan's gross monthly income was decreased by $225 per month, her mortgage will have been fully paid off at age 60.

For ages 70 through 90, Susan plans to continue to receive distributions from her 457(b) plan and receive her Social Security Retirement benefit. By delaying her Social Security Retirement benefit, Susan was able to take full advantage of the delayed retirement credits. Susan will pay federal tax on the 457(b) distributions, but she will not have to pay NYS taxes, because she will continue to take advantage of the $20,000 NYS Pension/Annuity Exclusion. The Social Security Retirement benefit will be 85% taxable by the federal government, but it will not be taxed by NYS. Susan will have the following retirement funds to use from age 70 to 90:

1. $4,429 monthly pension benefit
2. $1,275 monthly distribution from the NYCDCP 457(b) plan
3. $2,200 monthly Social Security Retirement benefit
4. $12,000 annual VSF payment
   - Total annual gross income before-tax: $94,850
   - Total monthly gross income before-tax: $7,904

Susan's retirement planning is straightforward, but she was able to take advantage of the no 10% early distribution penalty 401(k) plan (age 50 rule) and, at the same time, avoid or limit NYS taxes on the 401(k) distributions. She also was able to leave her 457(b) invested for a ten-year period to achieve account appreciation. Additionally, Susan was able to take advantage of the Social Security delayed retirement credit provision for her to maximize her Social Security Retirement benefit.

Case Study #5 – Multiple Retirement Plans Distribution

Case study #5 reviews a NYPD retiree, Edward, who needs a significant distribution and has multiple retirement plans to choose from. The case study is presented to review the importance of understanding both the distribution rules and tax rules of various retirement plans.

Chapter 11: Case Studies

Background

Edward
- Retirement & IRS age = 50
- Currently 53 years old
- Resides in Putnam County New York
- Annual pension benefit = $50,000
- Annual VSF benefit = $12,000
- NYCDCP 457(b) balance = $275,000
- NYCDCP Roth 401(k) balance = $125,000
- NYCDCP Special 401(k) balance = $170,000
- IRA = $80,000
- Roth IRA = $60,000

When Edward retired, he elected a final withdrawal of $150,000 from the NYCPPF, which he rolled over to the NYCDCP Special 401(k) plan. The Special 401(k) plan has appreciated to $170,000 over the three years Edward has been retired. Edward's Roth 401(k) plan consists of $90,000 of after-tax contributions and $35,000 of earnings/appreciation. Edward's Roth IRA consists of $40,000 of annual contributions and $20,000 of earnings/appreciation. Edward's IRA consists of before-tax money and is from a 401(k) rollover from an employer before his NYPD job.

Years ago, Edward purchased land in Adirondack State Park, and now he would like to build a cabin on the land. Edward does not want a mortgage and estimates he will need $300,000 to build the cabin. Additionally, Edward is single and does not have a desire to leave any of his money to a beneficiary upon his death. Based on his five retirement plans, Edward needs to determine the most tax-efficient method, at both the federal and NYS level, to distribute the $300,000. Edward is trying to decide based on three different scenarios.

Scenario #1
- Distribute $160,000 from the NYCDCP 457(b) plan
- Distribute $80,000 from the IRA
- Distribute $60,000 from the Roth IRA

Table #66 displays the federal and NYS income tax results for tax year 2018.

TABLE #66		
Case Study #5-1		
Item	Federal	NYS
Pension benefit	$50,000	$50,000
VSF	$12,000	$12,000
457(b) distribution	$160,000	$160,000
IRA distribution	$80,000	$80,000
Roth IRA distribution*	$20,000	$20,000
Adjusted Gross Income	$322,000	$322,000
NYS full pension exclusion	N/A	-$62,000
Standard deduction	-$12,000	-$8,000
Taxable income	$310,000	$252,000
Tax	$84,190	$17,197
10% penalty tax	$10,000	N/A
Total taxes	$94,190	$17,197

*The Roth IRA distribution consists of $40,000 in contributions (non-taxable) and $20,000 of earnings subject to taxation and penalty.

Scenario #2
- Distribute $260,000 from the NYCDCP 457(b) plan
- Distribute $40,000 from the Roth IRA*

*The Roth IRA distribution consists of $40,000 in contributions removed tax-free and penalty-free.

Chapter 11: Case Studies

Table #67 displays the federal and NYS income tax results for tax year 2018.

\multicolumn{3}{c}{TABLE #67}
\multicolumn{3}{c}{Case Study #5-2}
Item	Federal	NYS
Pension benefit	$50,000	$50,000
VSF	$12,000	$12,000
457(b) distribution	$260,000	$260,000
Adjusted Gross Income	$322,000	$322,000
NYS full pension exclusion	N/A	-$62,000
Standard deduction	-$12,000	-$8,000
Taxable income	$310,000	$252,000
Total taxes	$84,190	$17,197

Scenario #3
- Distribute $135,000 from the NYCDCP 457(b) plan
- Distribute $125,000 from the NYCDCP Roth 401(k) plan*
- Distribute $40,000 from the Roth IRA**

*The NYCDCP Roth 401(k) distribution is non-qualified and consists of $90,000 contributions removed tax-free and penalty-free (established for more than five years), $35,000 subject to taxation and 10% early distribution penalty.

**The Roth IRA distribution consists of $40,000 contributions removed tax-free and penalty-free.

Table #68 displays the federal and NYS income tax results for tax year 2018.

TABLE #68		
Case Study #5-3		
Item	*Federal*	*NYS*
Pension benefit	$50,000	$50,000
VSF	$12,000	$12,000
457(b) distribution	$135,000	$135,000
Roth 401(k) distribution	$35,000	$35,000
Adjusted Gross Income	$232,000	$232,000
NYS full pension exclusion	N/A	-$62,000
Standard deduction	-$12,000	-$8,000
Taxable income	$220,000	$162,000
Tax	$52,690	$10,138
10% penalty tax	$3,500	N/A
Total taxes	$56,190	$10,138

Recommended Strategy

Although scenario #3 appears to be the most favorable, Edward has another scenario that would significantly reduce his tax liabilities. The following is the recommended strategy for Edward.

> - Roll over the entire NYCDCP Roth 401(k) plan to his Roth IRA
> - Distribute $170,000 from the NYCDCP 401(k) plan
> - Distribute $130,000 from the Roth IRA*
>
> *After Edward rolls over the NYCDCP Roth 401(k) plan to his Roth IRA, he can remove $130,000 tax-free and penalty-free from the Roth IRA.

Chapter 11: Case Studies

Table #69 displays the federal and NYS income tax results for tax year 2018.

TABLE #69		
Case Study #5-4		
Item	Federal	NYS
Pension benefit	$50,000	$50,000
VSF	$12,000	$12,000
Special 401(k) distribution	$170,000	$170,000
Adjusted Gross Income	$232,000	$232,000
NYS full pension exclusion	N/A	-$211,600
Standard deduction	-$12,000	-$8,000
Taxable income	$220,000	$12,400
Tax	$52,690	$516

Case Study #6 – Terminal Leave & Age 50

Case study #6 reviews a NYPD pre-retiree, Elizabeth, who is planning to take her terminal leave (stay on payroll) to reach an IRS defined retirement age of 50. Elizabeth wants the ability to receive distributions from her various retirement plans without the 10% early distribution penalty. Elizabeth plans to use a three consecutive calendar year average when calculating her pension.

Background

Elizabeth
- DOB = 10/01/1970
- Retirement date "cashing-out" terminal leave = 11/30/2019
- Retirement date taking terminal leave = 02/15/2020
- NYCPPF retirement age = 49
- IRS retirement age = 50

Assumptions (retirement date of 11/30/2019
- Annual pension = $75,000
- ASF balance = $300,000
- Assumptions (retirement date of 02/15/2020
- Annual pension = $75,620
- ASF balance = $306,000

Analysis

Even though the NYCPPF will use a retirement age of 49, Elizabeth will satisfy the IRS age of 50 if her retirement date is any time after 01/01/2020. NYCPPF defines age using the closest birthday, while the IRS defines age as the age you are turning in the calendar year. Table #70 displays the result of Elizabeth's breakeven analysis ignoring finalization.

\multicolumn{4}{c	}{**TABLE #70**}
\multicolumn{4}{c	}{**Terminal Leave Break-even Analysis (Elizabeth)**}
Retirement months/years	TL Lump Sum	TL Stay on Payroll	Result
Monthly pension	$6,250	$0	-$6,250
Monthly pension	$6,250	$0	-$12,500
½ Monthly pension	$3,125	$0	-$15,625
1	$75,000	$75,620	-$15,005
2	$75,000	$75,620	-$14,385
3	$75,000	$75,620	-$13,765
4	$75,000	$75,620	-$13,145
5	$75,000	$75,620	-$12,525
6	$75,000	$75,620	-$11,905
7	$75,000	$75,620	-$11,285
8	$75,000	$75,620	-$10,665
9	$75,000	$75,620	-$10,045
10	$75,000	$75,620	-$9,425
11	$75,000	$75,620	-$8,805
12	$75,000	$75,620	-$8,185
13	$75,000	$75,620	-$7,565
14	$75,000	$75,620	-$6,945
15	$75,000	$75,620	-$6,325
16	$75,000	$75,620	-$5,705
17	$75,000	$75,620	-$5,085
18	$75,000	$75,620	-$4,465
19	$75,000	$75,620	-$3,845
20	$75,000	$75,620	-$3,225

Chapter 11: Case Studies

Retirement months/years	TL Lump Sum	TL Stay on Payroll	Result
21	$75,000	$75,620	-$2,605
22	$75,000	$75,620	-$1,985
23	$75,000	$75,620	-$1,365
24	$75,000	$75,620	-$745
25	$75,000	$75,620	-$125
26	$75,000	$75,620	+$495
Total	$1,965,625	$1,966,120	

Reviewing table #70 indicates that it takes Elizabeth approximately 26 years to break-even regarding the decision to take her terminal leave (stay on payroll). Elizabeth's annual pension increased by $620 due to remaining on payroll and she was able to reach the IRS retirement age of 50.

About the Author

Peter Thomann, EA, CFP®, CDFA® is the owner of Thomann Tax, Inc., a tax preparation and pension/retirement/divorce consulting firm located in Staten Island, NY. The firm specializes in the unique tax, pension, retirement, and divorce issues of active and retired NYC employees (FDNY, NYPD, Teachers, Sanitation, Corrections, etc.). Thomann is an Enrolled Agent, Certified Financial Planner®, Certified Divorce Financial Analyst®, holds a master's degree in financial planning, and a bachelor's degree in accounting. Thomann has years of experience helping clients with tax preparation, tax planning, retirement planning strategies, and has been a featured speaker at retirement planning seminars and training sessions.

Made in the USA
Middletown, DE
06 July 2025